SCOTTISH MOUNTAINEERING CLUB
DISTRICT GUIDE BOOKS

THE
Central Highlands

by Peter Hodgkiss

THE SCOTTISH MOUNTAINEERING CLUB
EDINBURGH

First published in Great Britain in 1984 by
THE SCOTTISH MOUNTAINEERING CLUB

First Edition   1934
Second Edition   1952
Third Edition   1968
Fourth Edition   1984

ISBN 0 907521 06 1

Filmset by Advanced Filmsetters (Glasgow) Ltd
Printed by Brown Son & Ferguson Ltd
Bound by James Gowans Ltd

FOREWORD

Mountains are often solemnised as being eternal, whereas mountain guide books are perpetually in a state of flux. This latest production conforms to the normal mould in its reconsideration of the mountains of Central Scotland, a region highly attractive to all sorts of visitors. A problem region to an author trying to maintain a harmonious balance between the high lights of Glen Coe, Nevis, Ben Alder and Creag Meagaidh and the muted tones of the Monadh Liath and Drumochter Hills.

Changes in roads, tracks, maps, estates, transport, afforestation and access in general are noted. New climbs, or selected climbs, not included in the appropriate Rock and Ice Guide Book Series are indicated. An appreciation of the individual qualities of the mountains comprising the different sections proffers informative details useful to hill walkers, rock climbers (summer and winter), cross country skiers and perchance even those who aspire to new routes.

Throughout the main aim has been clarity. Added to the central concern of mountain description the author has interwoven a wide range of comment and observation over a wide range of related topics of interest to the mountaineer out and about on the hills. With a full set of excellent photographs Peter Hodgkiss has produced a most valuable contribution to this series.

ALEX C. D. SMALL

CONTENTS

MAPS AND DIAGRAMS

drawn by James Renny
diagram 13 drawn by John MacKenzie

ILLUSTRATIONS

ACKNOWLEDGEMENTS

Many people have helped me in the production of this edition. For information I want to thank Alan Fyffe, John Grant, Ron Hockey, John Miller, Tom Rigg, Klaus Schwartz, Mike Thornley, the staff of the Scottish Landowners' Federation, and the staff at the Forestry Commission in Glasgow. Christine Mill allowed me to use information from her biography of Norman Collie (waiting publication).

The SMC Journal in its 32 volumes has been an invaluable source as have of course the two previous editions of this guide by Harry MacRobert and Campbell R. Steven. Jim Renny has drawn specially all the maps which lend clarity to the guide and several photographers (acknowledged in the captions) have helped with illustrations. I am grateful to John MacKenzie for the fine drawing he made of the crag on Chno Dearg; also to Paul Hodgkiss for the tailpiece of Ben Alder Cottage.

My warm thanks go to Robert Aitken who has provided a constant and ready flow of reference material, to Scott Johnstone who has been unstinting with photographic help and advice about geological matters, and to Alex Small who has been a patient and constructive editor.

Finally my heartfelt gratitude goes to my wife Joy who has been a willing typist and a good companion on the hill.

PREFACE

It is wholly appropriate that this guide should begin with a brief account of a traverse from Dalwhinnie to Inveroran that almost bisected the Central Highlands. William Naismith and Gilbert Thomson, two of the rocks on which the SMC was founded, had been dissatisfied with the time taken and their state of near exhaustion after a traverse from Clachaig to the Kingshouse over Bidean, Buachaille Etive Beag and Buachaille Etive Mór and concluding that lack of calories had been the major debilitating factor they undertook to reach the 1892 Easter meet of the SMC at Inveroran from Dalwhinnie carrying sufficient food to enable them to arrive fresh. Starting from Glasgow on the overnight train, they left Dalwhinnie at 3.30 am on April 14th crossed Ben Alder by the Short Leachas and by descent of its south ridge to Ben Alder Cottage, forded the River Gaur at Dunan, and then marched near the present line of the West Highland Railway to finish by fording the Orchy at its outlet from Loch Tulla. They arrived at Inveroran by 8.00 pm having walked 41 miles, yet still with food left, and fresh enough to enjoy dinner, and to be out on the hills on the following day when Naismith led an ascent of the Upper Couloir on Stob Ghabhar.

Changes there certainly have been since these two stalwarts strode from Atholl to Glenorchy—no longer could one hope for hospitality at Ben Alder Cottage or Gorton, both now open bothies; and the railway, afforestation and hydroelectricity have all left their mark—but anyone wishing to emulate Naismith and Thomson would cross the same exhilarating mountain, encounter the same bogs, and would still have to ford the Orchy to save being an hour late for dinner at Inveroran. All those who enjoy that sense of wilderness, still to be enjoyed in most parts of the Central Highlands, would do well to be both vigilant and active in protection of that value.

INTRODUCTION

Area

The area of the Central Highlands is clearly demarcated within the lines made to the west by Loch Linnhe and the Great Glen, and to the east by the A9. To the south a more broken line follows Loch Etive into the Pass of Brander and beyond it to swing north up Glen Orchy and along the West Highland Railway to Rannoch Station, where it turns east along the B846 to reach the A9.

Within the area there are 74 hills of over 914.4 m (3000 ft) complying with Sir Hugh Munro's list, and these are identified in their chapter headings by use of an asterisk. In addition there are a similar number of tops subsidiary to the main hills and over 40 separate hills exceeding 762 m (2500 ft).

Transport

For those who do not wish to travel by car, and also as an extension to private transport, the Central Highlands are served by three railway lines; the most important of these being the West Highland Railway which runs throughout the year, Sundays excepted, between Glasgow and Fort William and provides access to one of the most remote areas in Scotland. Starting at 6.00 am from Glasgow or after a leisurely breakfast at Bridge of Orchy, one can enjoy a day's hillwalking on the hills about Loch Ossian and a fast-moving party can make the round-trip from Corrour Halt to Ben Alder in between the morning and evening trains. Distances between the stations on this line seem almost designed for hill traverses and allow one to leave the morning train at say Corrour and to walk across the hills to either Rannoch or Tulloch for the evening train.

From that part of the line between Crannach Wood and the Blackwater, the view across Rannoch Moor on a clear winter's day is breathtaking. Particularly if there be no snow on the moor, its vast, brown expanse with a black-cloth of white, jaggy peaks gives a marvellous sense of distance and of magnitude to the distant hills of the Black Mount and Glencoe.

Of lesser importance to the Central Highlands are the lines to Oban and to Inverness. The latter provides access at Dalwhinnie to the Ben Alder group and to the Drumochter Hills, and, at Newtonmore to the Monadh Liadhs; while the former can be used to approach the Cruachan range from Dalmally or Loch Etive from Taynuilt.

Though not fitted for travel to and from the hills in a day from the main Scottish conurbations, bus services on all the main roads in and around the periphery of the Central Highlands add greatly to the flexibility of travel and enable the car-less hill-goer to reach some very remote corners. One can for example penetrate the north-eastern fringes of the Monadh Liadhs by the bus—a 4-seater land-rover—from Tomatin to Coignafearn; or, use the local service plying between Fort William and Glen Nevis (July and August only) to save one's feet from the tarmac at the end of a traverse from Corrour Halt.

Another way of extending freedom of movement in one part of the area is to make use of the steamer that plies up and down Loch Etive between Easter and end-September. This service runs from Auchnacloich, which is a few km west of Taynuilt and there are two sailings each day of the week, Sundays included, at approximately 10.15 am and 2.05 pm. Normally passengers make the round-trip but prior arrangement can be made for a party to be put off at Kinlochetive or possibly at Barrs or Armaddy. Phone Taynuilt 280 (STD Code 08662).

An essential reference work is the publication of the Highlands and Islands Development Board entitled *Getting around the Highlands and Islands* which is, as it claims, a comprehensive guide and shows the intriguing possibilities for long hill-traverses aided by a conjunction of train and bus (with or without a car).

Access

Outside the stalking season (mid-August to mid-October) there should be no problem with right of access, but during this period the estates do rely on lets of stalking to produce much of their income and unrestricted access would not be compatible with successful stalking. That said, a courteous approach to the estate in question from small parties of hill-goers, either by phone on the evening prior to the planned hill-walk or in person before setting out on the hill, will rarely meet with a blanket refusal. Such parties will more than probably be asked to avoid certain stretches of hill or particular glens and corries, but again the probability is that constructive suggestions as to alternative expeditions will be offered. However it is difficult for estates to accommodate large parties on the hills at this time and it would be diplomatic for clubs to organise their meets during the period to areas not carrying deer or to others owned by the National Trust. The representative body for estate owners, The Scottish Landowners' Federation, have shown a most cooperative attitude towards approaches from the Mountaineering Council of Scotland and have been constructive in making this guide-book more informative, providing freely details as to estate boundaries and local contacts. With regard to the bothies owned by the estates and left open for use by hill-goers, access to small parties *outside the stalking season*, presents no problem but any party in excess of 4 planning use of a bothy for 2 nights and more should seek permission from the estate factor or stalker.

There follows a list of estates in the Central Highlands including addresses and telephone numbers of the local contacts. Reference to the end paper map will show the boundaries of each estate and therefore the hills lying within each.

It has proved impracticable to include each and every parcel of land in the Central Highlands in this list and a notable exception is that land owned by the Forestry Commission. Here the recent instruction from Westminster to sell substantial amounts of land has made the situation too changeable for worthwhile inclusion. However most of the major estates are listed and certainly all those containing major hill groups set in deer forests.

Estate	Hills	Factor— telephone	Stalker— local contact
Glen Creran	Beinn Sgulaird	0631 63617	Mr. G. Livingstone 063 173 312
Glen Kinglass	Beinn nan Aighenan	0631 63617	Mr. T. Healy 086 62 271
Crunachy	West end of Cruachan	0631 63617	Mr. T. Healy 086 62 271
Glen Strae	Beinn Mhic Mhonaidh	0631 63617	Mr. A. MacLeod 083 82 217
Dalness	Meall nan Eun, Stob Coir' an Albannaich	0631 63617	Mr. A. Hunter 085 56 252
Ardchattan	Creach Bheinn	Bonawe 274	————
Black Mount	Clach Leathad	————	Mr. H. Menzies 083 84 225 or Mr. I. MacRae 083 84 269
Glen Etive (part of Black Mount)	Ben Starav	————	Mr. J. Fraser 085 56 277
Black Corries	Beinn a' Chrulaiste	————	Mr. J. White 085 56 272
*BACO Mamore	All the Mamores	0937 2411	Mr. W. Loudon 085 54 337
*BACO Killiechonate	Ben Nevis; all the Grey Corries	0937 2411	Mr. D. MacKinnon 039 781 204
Pollok and Corrour	Leum Uilleim, Chno Dearg	01 352 7637	Mr. Moffat— no phone. House at head of Loch Ossian.
Dunan	Beinn Pharlagain	0908501 252	No phone. Dunan Lodge, by Rannoch station.
Camusericht (Rannoch AG)	Sgor Gaibhre, Sgor Choinnich	Cortachy 222	Mr. D. Stewart 088 23 207
Ben Alder	Ben Alder, Culra and Ben Alder Bothies	————	Mr. T. Oswald 052 82 224
Laggan-Ardverikie	Beinn a' Chlachair Blackburn Bothy	052 83 200	————
Fountain Forestry	Creag Meagaidh	0463 224 948	————
North Drumochter	A'Mharconaich	————	Mr. A. Anderson 052 82 224
Craiganour Forest	Route from Loch Rannoch to Loch Garry	0887 20496	Mr. H. Littlejohn 088 22 324
Coire Bhachaidh (Rannoch AG)	Beinn Udlamain	————	Mr. D. Stewart 088 23 207
Pitmain	Route from Kingussie to Tomatin	0887 20496	Mr. W. Dey 05402 237
Glen Roy	Hills on either side of the glen	————	Mr. R. J. Japp 039 781 210

* Preferable to phone Factor.

Accommodation

Anyone wishing to spend time in the more remote parts of the Central Highlands will need either to carry a tent or to make overnight use of the bothies left open by the various estates. In most cases the Mountain Bothies Association help to maintain these bothies, and this organisation has done much to engender good relationships between landowners and hill-goers. Otherwise the area is well served by hotels, guest-houses, bed and breakfast houses and youth hostels. Then there is the possibility of informal arrangements for accommodation in some of the remote farms, and here a diplomatic approach on the spot can often produce heart-warming results. Details of official camp and caravan sites, youth hostels, mountaineering club huts and other accommodation are given in the relevant chapters. There follows a short list of useful addresses and publications.

1. Mountain Bothies Association—General Secretary
      Richard Genner
      42, Lamberton Court,
      Pencaitland,
      East Lothian.

2. Scottish Youth Hostels Association
      7, Glebe Crescent,
      Stirling FK8 2JA.

3. Getting around the Highlands and Islands (pub. HIDB) from
      Highlands and Islands Development Board
      27, Bank Street.
      Inverness IV1 1QR.

4. Where to stay in Scotland
      Self Catering Accommodation in Scotland,
      Scottish Tourist Board,
      Ravelston Terrace,
      Edinburgh, EA4 3EU.

Maps

The current source of information concerning heights, distances and Gaelic spelling, used in this guide is the O.S. 1:50,000 First and Second Series: only occasionally has recourse been made to the O.S. 1:25,000 (Pathfinder Series and Second Series) for spot heights and lesser physical detail. Five of the 1:50,000 First and

Second Series—Nos. 34, 41, 42, 50 and 52—cover almost the whole of the Central Highlands, with only the coastal strip of Benderloch and Appin and the northernmost triangle between the Great Glen and the A9, missing.

While admiring the clarity of the 1:50,000 Second Series and the thoroughness with which their content has been metricated, one can regret the demise of the O.S. One inch to One Mile Sheet 47 covering the heart of the Central Highlands and including Ben Nevis, Ben Alder, Glencoe and Stob Ghabhar. That said the Ordnance Survey's latest 1:50,000 maps have the decided advantage of later revision—variously between 1974 and 1980; they contain paths additional to the previous one inch to one mile series, and other new information such as the extended boundaries of afforestation. With regard to this latter subject, the 1:25,000 maps have particular value, showing access tracks, paths and cuttings through afforestation, that are not included in the 1:50,000 maps. Additionally the 1:25,000 Pathfinder Series have generally an even later revision date than the 1:50,000 maps and include greater detail as to features such as waterfalls and the siting of named crags.

For convenience on the hill, the 1:50,000 maps are unmatchable and can only be improved by marking in such detail from the 1:25,000 as is considered relevant to individual needs.

Rock, Snow and Ice Climbing

Those who come to the Central Highlands intent on more than general mountaineering will want the specialist publications of the SMC—A. C. Stead's *Lochaber and Badenoch*, K. V. Crockett's *Glencoe* and J. R. Marshall's *Ben Nevis*, the two former being selective guides to all the major mountain crags in the district and the latter a comprehensive guide to Nevis with a supplement on Polldubh. This edition will not describe other than the occasional classic route in the well-known climbing areas but does give detail for the lesser known crags not described in the three guides above. These crags are generally remote and contain few routes, but their quality lies in their very remoteness and in the sense of exploration still to be enjoyed.

Gradings do not include routes harder than Very Severe, but it is worth making the point that a 200 m Severe fully 2 hours walk from the road and usually containing pitches lubricated by seepage, is a more serious proposition than a route of similar length and technical difficulty reached in 30 minutes and cleaned by regular traffic to the point where the rock is sound and dry. Winter gradings are as follows.

Grade I—Straightforward, averaged-angled snow gullies, generally showing no pitches under adequate snow cover. They may, however, present cornice difficulty.

Grade II—Pitches encountered in gullies, or gullies with high-angled or difficult cornice exits. The easier buttresses which under snow present more continuous difficulty.

Grade III—Serious climbs which should only be undertaken by parties with good experience. Reaches technical standard of Severe.

Grade IV—Routes which are either of sustained Severe standard or climbs of higher difficulty which are too short to be classed as Grade V.

Grade V—Routes which give major expeditions and are only to be climbed when conditions are favourable. Technical standard Very Severe.

In this guide, winter gradings are deliberately biased in that the hardest conditions are assumed. An example would be Tower Ridge, Grade III, which in pleasant spring weather is often straightforward enough to become a well-tramped highway, but which can just as often present pitches of technical difficulty equivalent to the Severe rock-climbing standard when for instance ice-bulges form at the Little Tower.

The Scottish Mountaineering Club Journal, published annually, is a useful source of additional information about mountaineering in the area covered by this guide and particularly about new routes and first ascents, significant changes in mountain shelters, bridges, paths and general access, as well as alterations to designated mountain heights and the status of Munros.

Ski-ing

The piste slopes on Meall a'Bhuiridh are sufficiently mechanised to allow a day of frequent runs but have yet retained an air of informality and low density that is perhaps a reflection of the fickle weather in the west.

Mountain skiers will find a great variety of usually long expeditions where either the use of two cars at each end of a traverse—as with the crossing of Meall a'Bhuiridh and Stob Ghabhar—or use of the West Highland Line—say for the traverse from Corrour over Ben na Lap and Stob Coire Sgriodain to Tulloch—is of great advantage. Creag Meagaidh remains unsullied by mechanisation and, with its great bulk and numerous corries, offers more mountain ski-ing than most other hills in the Central Highlands. Other notable catchment areas are described in their relevant chapters.

Avalanches and Rock-fall

The growing number of people going out on the Scottish hills in winter has brought a greater appreciation of the frequency and scale of avalanches. There is no doubt that avalanches of most types occur frequently in Scotland and, the sceptics, who would not acknowledge the serious danger of Scottish avalanches, have retreated in the last decade under the weight of evidence. Anyone intending even simple winter hill-walks in the Central Highlands would do well to read one of the standard texts on this subject (see below) and to absorb knowledge of the more predictable avalanche conditions. Then close attention to weather forecasts and to weather changes during the course of a hill-day are equally important. For those intending to climb one of the snow and ice routes, and particularly one of the gullies, a thermometer is a worthwhile adjunct to winter climbing equipment. From knowledge gained by reading about avalanches and from observation, avoidance of the more obvious hazards, such as a cornice in thaw conditions, is a straightforward matter. It is in avoidance of the less predictable that the trick (and a certain amount of luck) lies, and in this context it is well to remember that the seeming extreme examples of slab avalanches occurring at angles of 15° and of parties being engulfed on much-frequented paths, have both caused fatalities in the last few winters (both in the Allt a' Mhuillin).

A last, sobering thought on this subject, is that there is a concensus among those who have studied and written about the phenomenon, that a certain percentage of avalanches (some put it at 30%) is not predictable in the state of present knowledge.

1. Avalanche Enigma   C. Fraser, Murray
2. Avalanche Handbook   R. I. Perla and M. Martinelli, Jr.,
                                 U.S. Dept. of Agriculture
3. SMCJ—XXXII No. 172 Two articles by R. G. W. Ward
        XXXI No. 170 Statistical article by Blyth Wright
        XXXI No. 168 Snaba's by Roger O'Donovan
4. Mountain Leadership   E. Langmuir, Scottish Sports
                                 Council

Rock-fall

Though not in the same order of occurrence as avalanches, rock-fall as an objective danger during scrambling should be guarded against. Numbers have again brought a hitherto un-recognised problem to light, both as initiating agents on the ridge above one and in terms of increased observation. On some of the easier rockclimbs on Ben Nevis (Observatory Ridge) and on Buachaille Etive Mor (North Buttress) several incidents have been reported in the last few years.

Weather

The Central Highlands has a higher rainfall than most areas in the United Kingdom with only a belt of land west of the Great Glen recording greater precipitation. That said the climatic variation over a distance from west to east of only 50 km is wide, as is shown by the following mean figures drawn from a publication by the Meteorological Office in Edinburgh.

         1941–70 *Rainfall*
         Glen Etive and Glencoe—more than 3200 mm pa.
         Eastern Rannoch   —less than 1600 mm pa.
or   *Snow lying at 9.00 am*
         Glencoe   50% coverage; valley observation 20 days.
         Ben Alder 50% coverage; valley observation 60 days.
and   *Temperature—January minimum*
         Glencoe at 1000 m $-4°C$
         Ben Alder at 1000 m $-6°C$.

Much of the weather is of Atlantic origin with the mild, moisture-bearing south-westerlies seeming more predominant than is the case: almost as much wind comes from the south-east quadrant and consistent south-easterlies when not carrying rain will produce strong haze making it difficult to see the outline of hills only a few kilometres away even when there is blue sky above. North-westerlies are also frequent and normally bring a lowering of temperature, blustery showers and, in between, excellent visibility. The stable conditions of an anti-cyclone are often of short duration and those that last for longer periods, usually in association with blocking zones of high pressure over Scandinavia, are recalled in revered tones at climbing club dinners. Another anti-cyclonic condition even more infrequent is that where the usual altitudinal temperature gradient becomes inverted and air sinks into the glens to form a cloud-sea, while the tops remain clear in cool and dry conditions: to be on a mountain ridge on such a day is a unique and heady experience, more especially so if the Moor of Rannoch be close enough for the blanket of cloud to suggest the one-time glacial ice-dome.

Limited to weekends, climbers have little choice in the matter of weather, which is therefore of some fascination and careful consideration of the alternatives can be repaying. One example would be when south-westerlies prevail and a day of infrequent showers could be spent on the Drumochter hills when Cruachan is blattered with those 'frequent showers' of the meteorological forecast that are, on the hill, indistinguishable from continuous rain. Another example might be the rarer condition when more notable variations occur in association with zones of low pressure moving across Southern England: the northern fringes of such zones can be significant to relatively small areas and thus Cruachan can be under heavy cloud while Creag Meagaidh enjoys clear skies.

A too obsessional consideration of weather can be unrewarding, but regular study of radio forecast and of weather reports from coastal stations, allied to personal observation, is worthwhile. From such attention over the past 15 years, two patterns have been regular—a period of low temperature often accompanied by snowfall in late November and a subsequent thaw in the path of south-westerlies in time for the holiday period at the end of December!

A good reference work is Gordon Manley's *Climate and the British Scene* (Fontana New Naturalist) and for its fascinating insight into the life of the meteorologists in the Ben Nevis

Observatory around the turn of the century as much as for its weather data, William T. Kilgour's *Twenty Years on Ben Nevis* is a good read. Though out of print for some decades, the public library service should find a copy for the determined enquirer.

History, Human

Man's presence on and among the hills of the Central Highlands is well documented only in recent historical times. Gaelic, the sole language of the Central Highlands until the 18th century had no written history—indeed its first book, known as Carswell's 'Liturgy', did not appear until 1567 and though its oral tradition is accepted as an art form, it is not viewed as historically reliable.

The higher reaches of the glens have been used for centuries by pastoralists and evidence of their summer residence can be seen in the 'rickle heap stane' remaining from shielings and in Gaelic names such as 'airidh' (shieling) or 'blar' (a cleared space), both often found in names for places deep in the recesses of the hills. Evidence of man as a hunter on the hills is also found in Gaelic, there being innumerable references to 'eilde' (hind), 'gaibhre' (goat), 'daimh' (stag) and other prey in names of hill-form. However the great Caledonian forest of red pine would have been an enormous hindrance to either activity until it was cleared by felling and burning, a process that did not commence until the 1st century A.D.

Those activities that have been well described are related to warfare, commerce, road and rail building. From these a personal selection that seems particularly relevant to man's movement on and through the hills starts and with pride of place, with the awe-inspiring night crossing in winter of the hills between the Great Glen and Glen Spean by Montrose and his small army of 1500 men. Early on the morning of 31st January 1645, Montrose started his band of Atholl, Appin and Glencoe clansmen together with Irish mercenaries and Camerons, on a flank march intending surprise as a weapon to defeat opposing forces more than four times the number of his own, that were gathered north and south of him in the Great Glen. They struck south up Glen Tarff and over a bealach of 620 m to descend Glens Turret and Roy, not reaching Glen Spean until the morning of 1st February.

11

There was then a further 13 miles, skirting the hills on the south of the glen, to reach the base of Meall-an-t'Suidhe, where the clansmen soaked their plaids in water in order that they should be more wind-proof for their night's rest in the snow. This epic march is well described by John Buchan in his biography of Montrose (O.P.).

Another group of men who tackled the rigours of long journeys on foot were the drovers who brought their beasts for sale at the trysts of Falkirk and Crieff. By 1840 great quantities of black cattle—c. 150,000—were being delivered annually to Falkirk Tryst alone. From Mull they used the Pass of Brander and Glen Lochy to Tyndrum; from the north-western glens they came over the passes of Corrieyairack and Drumochter to Dalnacardoch; and from Skye they cut directly across the grain of the Central Highlands either using the lines of weakness provided by Glen Spean and the Lairig Leacach and then skirting Luim Uilleam and the lochans that were used as the site of the present Blackwater, to cross to the Kingshouse by the bealach east of Beinn a' Chrulaiste, or, going over the Lairig Mor from Fort William to Kinlochleven and then the Devil's Staircase to Altnafeadh: both latter routes converged on Inveroran, which has become, through literature, the acme of droving stances. Dorothy Wordsworth would 'have given £20 to have been able to take a lively picture of it'—the concourse in the kitchen at Inveroran—and goes on to draw as lively a picture in words as anyone could wish (*A Tour in Scotland: 1803*; James Thin, Edinburgh, 1974). Another intriguing insight into droving customs is given in the descriptions by 19th century travellers of drover's dogs returning north alone to be fed at each stance by prior arrangement while the master took the easier route by sea from Glasgow to Oban or Fort William. The magnus opus on the subject of droving is A. R. B. Haldane's *The Drove Roads of Scotland* (Edinburgh University Press, 1968).

Following the drovers, the road-makers avoided some of their high passes and generally took more circuitous routes. Here again A. R. B. Haldane has written a fine book, *New Ways through the Glens* (Nelson, 1962), that is almost as much a tribute to three honest public servants—Messrs Telford, Rickman and Hope—as a masterly evocation of 19th century road-building. However the only significant new road in the Central Highlands in which the three had a part, was that from Fort William to Kingussie to be used about the turn of the century by Edinburgh based climbers such as Raeburn, Tough and Brown who took the overnight train to Dalwhinnie and cycled to Aberarder or Fort William for a day out on Creag Meagaidh or Ben Nevis. The main route through the Central Highlands from Tyndrum to Inverness arose much earlier with George Wade in the 18th century responsible for that part between Fort William and Inverness, as he was also for the road over the Corrieyairack. Considering the lack of resources other than men and hand implements, the speed with which some of these military roads were completed is remarkable. That from Dalwhinnie to Fort Augustus over the Corrieyairack took 500 men only the summer of 1731 for its 31 miles and several bridges. It took rather more men to construct the section between Loch Tulla and Kingshouse, there being a total of 1100 men camped on either side of the Black Mount in the summer of 1752 (when Wade had left Scotland and Caulfield was responsible for military road-building). Later travellers crossing the Black Mount, remarked on finding rocks engraved with regimental names.

More recently about the turn of the century, the railway, and especially the West Highland Line from Glasgow to Fort William, had some influence on the development of mountain-eering in the Central Highlands. Although stalwarts such as W. W. Naismith and W. Inglis Clark had made the approach to Ben Nevis by the steamer service plying between the Clyde and Fort William, it was not until the opening of the West Highland Line in 1894 that climbers made regular visits and it is notable that before the railway reached Fort William there were only two mountaineering routes on the mountain (Tower Ridge—descent 3rd September 1892 and North-east Buttress—ascent 6th September 1892; both by the brothers Hopkinson). Thereafter, by the end of the century eighteen more routes had been made on the mountain.

The building of the West Highland Line bred its own legends, the foremost of which was the attempted crossing in winter of the Moor of Rannoch from Loch Treig head to Inveroran by seven men, only one of whom had crossed the Moor before: of the rest one was the 60 year old factor to the Marquis of Breadalbane. Their intention was to examine the proposed

13

route, but not only did they intend to complete over 30 miles of the roughest going in the short span of January daylight, but had included in their itinerary a noon rendezvous at the River Gaur for a site inspection with the landowner. Not surprisingly they failed to reach Inveroran and spent most of the night in varying states of collapse on the Moor. Help eventually arrived from Gorton but one Macalpine, described in accounts of the time as 'stout, full-blooded, and loquacious', actually got the length of Barravourich, a mere 6 miles from his destination.

Before the line could be laid, stretches of moor between Rannoch Station and the rising ground 8 km to the south, plus further stretches to the north required substantial drainage after which a great trench was filled with ash and glacial till on a bottoming of brushwood and heather. A temporary, light railway was used to transport the spoil across the moor, and when one of the small engines in use was derailed at the wettest part of the moor, it sank 12 ft through the course of the night.

Thousands of navvies were involved in building the line; a large number from Ireland and Highlandmen from all parts including a contingent from the Western Highlands where a recognised destitution brought them the benefit of a one-way fare from the contractor. Fixed camps were built at intervals for the occasional recuperation of the navvies, who normally slept in hutting or 'turf-dwellings' along the line. At one such— Achallader Camp—the Marquis of Breadalbane presided over the Black Mount Literary Association set up to 'excite a spirit of inquiry combined with healthy amusement among men employed upon the West Highland Railway during the winter season'. Programmes comprising pianoforte selections, light vocals and a service of fruit and rules barring entry of 'intoxicated or swearing men' can have done little to capture such audiences.

And so the droving routes fell into disuse as Highland bred cattle and sheep were transported by train across the Moor of Rannoch by much the route surveyed for Telford in 1811 when looking for an improved route to the cattle trysts of Central Scotland.

Flora and Fauna

The Central Highlands contain mainly acid soils most of which are poorly drained so that blanket bog is common: in few places does the birch bring its golden glow to autumn and even rarer are the remaining stands of oak in occasional southern exposures.

In most seasons the Scottish hills present a subdued display of russets, olive greens, bleached oranges and purples, giving startling exception to the brilliant orange berries of the mountain ash and to the under-foot luminescence of the wine-red and orange in sphagnum moss. Only in early summer can one follow Principal Shairp's instruction to

'Stoop and see a lowlier kind,
Creeping milkwart, pink, white, blue,'

and find the bright tints of wild orchid and sea-pink, or see a southern hillside fresh with green, new shoots of bracken.

The climber ascends through indistinct stages of vegetation. Not often in the Central Highlands does one avoid the lower, boggy ground where the aroma of bog myrtle and the tattered fleece of cotton grass vie with sphagnum moss and purple moor grass. Above 300 m plants of the bog give way to grass heaths such as mat grass, deer grass and stiff sedge with heather more predominant on the eastern hills. Once on the tops the striking feature is the dwarf-like nature of all growth. Indeed those hill-goers not specifically interested in flora, will only notice the miniature forms when perhaps recumbant on the tops in sunny weather. Then one may examine the tiny antlers of stag's horn moss or on rarer occasions, usually in gravelly clearings, the china-pink flowers of moss-campion clustered several dozen in a green cushion of perhaps 20 cm diameter. This beautiful flower survives in the arctic conditions above 900 m by driving down a tap-root often greater in length than the diameter of its cushion. On the eastern tops of the district, blaeberry and crowberry are more common and mix with the tawny, Nardus grasslands. The autumn blaeberry presents another delight for the hill-goer, the succulence of its berries as much appreciated by birds as can be seen from the purple stain of their droppings on the rocks at this time of year. These berries seem to grow as large and sweet on northern slopes as on more sunny exposures.

In only a few places in the Central Highlands, can the hill-goer enjoy the variety that indigenous trees bring to landscape. By the 16th century, when Elizabeth I took fright at the inroads

15

being made into the deciduous woodlands of England and passed legislation, that forced the charcoal burners to pursue their pillage into Scotland, the vast Caledonian forest of Scots pine had already been laid waste by various human agencies. The Norse raiders almost by custom, as much as for any purpose of flushing out defenders, burnt vast tracts of timber and also culled material for boat-building. Their deprivations stretched well inland from the western sea-board and were continued by the war-faring Scottish clans. Then the smelting industry and next the land-clearance for the coming of the sheep culminated the destruction. Here and there remnants can be seen—oak-woods in Glen Creran, Scots pine beside Loch Tulla and birch above Loch Etive—but man can now move freely about the hills.

Fauna

Few city-dwellers are accustomed to watching a hill side for the tell-tale movement of a fox otherwise indistinguishable in his perfect camouflage, but the ever present red deer are readily seen from most hills in the Central Highlands. In the Black Mount and Corrour estates vast herds congregate in the corries and, when disturbed, their wonderfully light, flowing movements can enliven many a dreich day. A peculiarly autumn noise is the roaring of the stag in rut—at a distance often terminating in a gloomy, coughing, groan—while the hind has a short, clear bark used rarely to warn a grazing herd of an intruder. Other signs of deer are the wallows that stags and hinds use for the removal of parasites: a pit of wettish peat with a substantial piece of pine in its midst is the place favoured by the stag, who will churn the peat with his fore-feet and use the old trunk as a rubbing post. As with other wild animals, deer have an extraordinary awareness of weather change. Deer watchers have frequently noted an otherwise inexplicable large-scale movement of deer to low ground two to three days before the onset of heavy snow-fall.

With the exception of the blue (alpine) and brown hares few other quadrupeds will be seen by the casual observer. Very occasionally, walking up-wind and hidden by an intervening ridge, one might surprise a fox: otherwise only his winter tracks, often on high ridge, will be seen. Even rarer sightings at low level, will be had of stoat, weasel, pine marten, wild-cat and red squirrel, while there is a little enough forest in the Central Highlands for the roe deer to be much seen. Unlike the case with land beasts, many species of birds will be seen in the course of a hill-walk. Even in winter grouse, ptarmigan and snow buntings will enliven most days, the first rising lower on the hill, almost from under foot with its alarm-call of 'awah, awah, awah', and flocks of the latter on the tops wheeling and banking to show their white undersides. Then in spring and early summer on high and open ground, the mournful whistle of the golden plover will sometimes be heard. But it is surely the ptarmigan that is *the* bird of the tops: a native of Scotland, spending its whole year above 650 m, and relying so much on its camouflage that one frequently approaches within spitting distance before it breaks from cover and runs as often as not until choosing a take-off point allowing a gliding descent. In winter both cock and hen are white all over apart from their black tails and a black eye patch on the cock. When they have scooped out a lee hollow in the snow, either to shelter from high winds or to uncover the plants on which they feed, they become undetectable. In summer when their plumage changes to a mottle of grey and brown, they blend just as well against lichen-covered boulders. Their young also have great confidence in the camouflage of their plumage and will remain perfectly still while a camera is moved to within a metre, though the hen will be several yards away desperately dragging a wing. Ptarmigan shooting has been one of the hill-sports and whatever one's attitudes to such pastimes, grudging admiration must surely be accorded to the writer of an article years ago, who claimed that for the birds to have a sporting chance, they should be stalked until close enough to shoot with a hand-gun (a pistol). He was also of the opinion that a pair of stout, nailed shoes were essential for this activity.

Few of the raptorial birds will be seen: the buzzard's mewing call will be heard more often than it is seen and casual sightings of eagle are extremely rare. This splendid bird is highly intolerant of human activity near to its nesting site and as over 4 months is involved between the laying of eggs and the eaglets becoming fledged, the potential for disturbance is large. Of the migratory birds, greylag geese provide a splendid sight, and sound, during their April flight north, in echelon with the lead position changing frequently in strong, head-winds and the whirr of their pinions audible from as much as 100 m below.

In the wooded glens and on the loch-sides a much greater variety of bird-life can be readily seen—particularly this is the case in the Etive basin. Lapwing, curlew, sand-piper and oyster-catcher among the waders are common as are many of the passerines including the yellow-hammer, grey wagtail and wheatear. Those having the leisure to wander up the eastern shore of Loch Etive and stop to eat beside a burn, will be unlucky not to catch sight of a dipper. (On the same shore, with a detour to the headland north of Inverleiver Bay, grey seal can often be seen basking on the islets not 95 m out into the loch.)

Last under this heading a little must be said about those small creatures which, on a still, humid day in July and August, can try the humour of the most ardent hill-goer. Worst by far is the midge and it will be found at its most maddening density in poorly drained glens such as Glen Etive: indeed it is claimed that they were far less numerous before the glens were cleared of crofters who, with their need to drain the land for cultivation, removed much of the insect's habitat. There is certainly little mention of the midge—meanbh-chuileag (little fly)—in Gaelic lore, although Prince Charles Edward Stuart seems to have found them trying during his flight across the Central and Western Highlands. Various proprietary creams and lotions are sold as repellants in all Highland chemists. Many have an active constituent of di-methyl-phthalate and these can usually be applied to the skin. For increased protection some authorities recommend application of a repellant to clothing and these may contain chemicals unsuitable for use on the skin. One repellant that the author has found effective, though this is a relative term in this context, has the trade name of Autan; and, many people claim noticeable relief from the burning of Moskill in a tent. The midge is preyed upon by dragonflies, frogs, palmated newts and, in the midge's pupal stage, by trout—there would seem some argument for regarding all these predators as protected species!

Other pests lesser in numbers but more unpleasant in their individual effect are blood-sucking clegs, the bite from which causes painful swellings and sheep-ticks, another blood-sucker that burrows into the skin of humans and sheep alike.

Against midges and clegs, a hat with a drooping brim provides some relief. Those wishing to mount a campaign against these

1.   *Cruachan's Taynuilt peak gives fine distant views: to the West, Ben More on Mull stands out well.*
Peter Hodgkiss

2.   The 'Dalmally Horse-shoe' with, left of centre, the east ridge leading to Stob Garbh's summit clearly defined by sunlight and shade.   *Peter Hodgkiss.*

3.   Stob Garbh from the east ridge of Sron an Isean. The ridge rising from the left to Stob Garbh's summit and just picked out by sunlight, makes a fine winter route.   *Peter Hodgkiss*

4. *On the Cruachan ridge; approaching Drochaid Ghlas from the east.*   *Peter Hodgkiss*

5. From Beinn a' Chochuill, the north ridges of Drochaid Ghlas and Cruachan show well. On th

he sun-lit, east face of Stob Dearg carries fine winter climbing.   *Peter Hodgkiss*

6.   *The long summit ridge of Beinn a' Chochuill from Beinn Eunaich.*   *Peter Hodgkiss*

7. *The Cruachan Range through the bealach between Beinn Eunaich and Beinn a'*
Chochuill.   *Peter Hodgkiss*

8. The magnificent view up Loch Etive from the lowly top of A' Cruach above Glennoe Farm.
Peter Hodgkiss

pests could start by reading *Insecticide Resistance and Vector Control: 17th Report of the Expert Committee on Insecticides.* Technical Report, World Health Organisation, No. 433, 1970.

For those hill-goers who wish to acquire a little knowledge about what they see on the hills, perhaps the widest overview is provided by F. Fraser Darling and J. Morton Boyd's *The Highlands and Islands,* (Collins New Naturalist, 1969) which itself contains a comprehensive bibliography. To those wanting to know more about red deer is recommended F. Fraser Darling's fascinating study *A Herd of Red Deer,* first published in 1937 and with several other printings over the years (OUP, 1969).

Land-form

The Central Highlands are the remains of a great range that reared up 400 million years ago, was first planed down to a plateau and then dissected to give much the land-form that we see today. They are composed of ancient metamorphic rocks known as Dalradian schists that stretch in a great belt with a SW to NE bias and are only broken to any large extent by the intrusive granites of Cruachan, Etive and Rannoch though extrusions of volcanic rocks at Glencoe and Ben Nevis are of great interest for rock-climbing and have had impact on the local land-form. To the west and, to a lesser extent, to the south, the area is moated by valleys eroded along natural faults—the Great Glen and the Pass of Brander—while to the east the boundary follows the Dalradian trend of Glen Orchy and then, more prosaically, the West Highland Line to Rannoch Station, the B846 to Killicranckie and the A9 to Inverness. Though contained within a tall oblong leaning to the NE of only 150 km height this area shows a wonderful variety of hills from the jagged outline of Cruachan's granite in the south-west to the rolling plateau of the Monadhliadh's mica-schist in the north-east. In between, weather-resistant quartzite gives the distinctive sharp ridges of the Mamores and Grey Corries; the Etive granites show in cream-coloured slabs of great extent and roughness on both sides of the loch; and at the centre cauldron-extrusions of lava have left compact rocks and the dramatic structure of the Glencoe hills and of the northern cirque of Ben Nevis. Through it all run the ice-gouged faults with that SW to NE trend so apparent in Lochs Etive and Ericht.

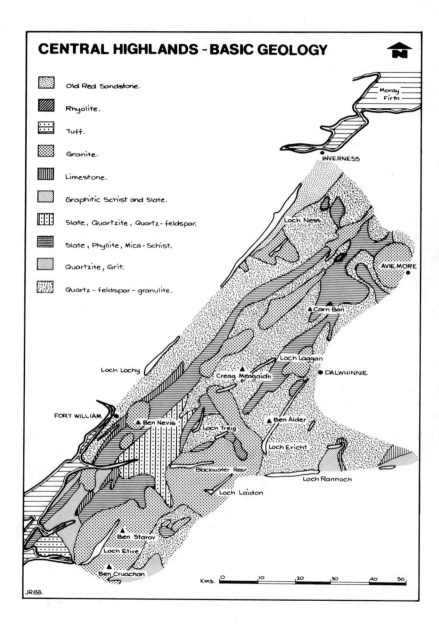

CENTRAL HIGHLANDS - BASIC GEOLOGY

Old Red Sandstone.

Rhyolite.

Tuff.

Granite.

Limestone.

Graphitic Schist and Slate.

Slate, Quartzite, Quartz-feldspar.

Slate, Phyllite, Mica-Schist.

Quartzite, Grit.

Quartz-feldspar-granulite.

Evidence of that effortless and most recent leveller—glaciation—is prominent on all sides, from the 'U' shaped valleys with truncated spurs and hanging coires, such as Glencoe itself, to the lesser but still evocative evidence in the furrows left as glaciation planed down the rock on the summit of Aonach Beag.

It is thought that the last remnant of the great Laggan-Spey glacier died c. 9000 yrs ago in the recess of Coire Leis and after a winter of heavy snowfall when on a day in May one may peer down 20 m into the bergschrund beneath Observatory Ridge, it needs little imagination to picture glaciation recurring with a slight deterioration in climate.

Those wishing a more than passing acquaintance with the land-form of the area would find the definitive text in A. Geike's *The Scenery of Scotland* (O.P.) with another, more accessible text in J. B. Whittow's *Geology and Scenery in Scotland* (Penguin, 1979). For those with some knowledge of geology G. S. Johnstone's *British Regional Geology—Scotland: The Grampian Highlands* (HMSO, 1966), contains much interest and a comprehensive bibliography.

Gaelic

One may walk and climb for years in the Scottish hills without any knowledge of Gaelic, or its pronunciation, and not feel the need of it. But a little insight into the Gaelic nomenclature of hill-forms will at least enrich one's knowledge of the environment, and can provide significant information, as in the case of 'Allt a' Mhuillin' (burn of the mill wheel), when one can be sure that during spring-melt or after heavy rain such a burn will run like a mill-race and will not be forded easily. Then avoidance of the more dissonant mispronunciations will help when seeking information from local people.

A very brief and selective glossary together with an indication as to the most glaring pitfalls in pronunciation, is given below. Those fortunate enough to live in Scotland can hear the 'clatter of Gaelic voices' as Ruthven Todd so well described it, on the VHF waveband on any evening of the week and, to especial advantage on Sunday afternoons when Gaelic services, with a primordial ring to their chanted responses, are broadcast on VHF by BBC Radio Scotland.

One of the characteristics of Gaelic nomenclature is the existence in the language of single words for hill-forms which, in English, could only be described by a multi-word phrase. An example is the noun 'druim' which might be briefly translated as a long, whale-back ridge, and such descriptive names for hill-forms are far more numerous than in English. But the Gaels never hesitate at using poetical groupings and nothing could be more descriptive than the Gaelic name for the dipper— 'Gobhainn dubh-a Chladaich' meaning the blacksmith of the shingle. In another vein there are curiosities illustrating a close familiarity with topography—Binnein Shuas and Binnein Shios in the Ardverikie Forest offer an example. The basic meaning for shuas is above (one) and that for shios is downwards (from one) with these two directions often referring to the flow of a burn and with their meanings extended to allow use of shuas for west and shios for east. A glance at sheet 42 of the O.S. 1:50,000 First Series will explain all; however, depending upon the predominant direction of the drainage in an area, the two words can be allotted to other opposing compass points!

When trying to relate Gaelic names to contour shapes on the map it can be helpful to remember that such names were given by people living and working on the lower slopes and rarely if ever from the higher vantage points.

In the following glossary, the phonetic script is based on a key by Iain and Iseabail MacLeod who are currently compiling a much larger glossary of Gaelic which is to be published in 1984 with the next edition of Munro's Tables. It is based on English spelling and it is therefore impossible to give other than a rough approximation of the Gaelic sounds, which are very different from those of English. This lack is also to some extent due to the variety of Gaelic pronunciation from region to region—there being no 'received' Gaelic. For instance Gaelic speakers in the Laggan area will say 'bellach' whereas across the Great Glen in Kintail 'byalach' is nearer the mark. However the key should enable the user to pronounce the names in such a way that they would be at least intelligible to a Gaelic speaker. Note that the script is based on the standard *Scottish* pronunciation and not on standard Southern English (for example, *day* and *road* have simple vowels and not diphthongs).

Vowels

a as in the
a   as in tap
aa as in father
ay as in day
ee as in deed, weak
i   as in tip
Y   as in by
o   as in top
oa as in road
aw as in bawl
oo as in pool
ou as in our
ow as in howl
ö approximately the sound in French oeuf or German Österreich

Consonants

Most of the consonants represent approximately the same sounds as in English, e.g.

g   as in get
s   as in sit
ch as in loch

gh has no equivalent in English; it is voiced ch (i.e. pronounce ch using the vocal chords).

y as in yet

^ indicates a slight y sound after a consonant
bold indicates the stressed syllable.

ban   —white, pale (baan)
beag   —little (bayk)
breac   —speckled (brechk)
buidhe   —yellow (b**oo**y*a*)
cas   —steep (cas)
dearg   —red (dyer*a*k)
dubh   —black (doo)
Fada   —long (**fat***a*)
fionn   —white, bright (fyoon)

garbh —rough (gar*a*v)
geal —white (gyal)
gearr —short (gyar)
glas —grey, green (glas)
gorm —blue (**gor***a*m)
labhar —loud (**lav***a*r)
liadh —grey (**lyee***a*)
mor —large (moar)
odhar —dun-coloured (**ou***a*r)
riabhach—brindled or striped (**ree***a*vach)
ruadh —ruddy-coloured (**roo***a*gh)
uaine —green, pallid (oo*a*ny*a*)

adharcan —lapwing (**ogh***a*rk*a*n)
ba —cattle (baa)
beith —birch (bay)
caorach —sheep (plural) (**kor**eech)
caorunn —rowan (k*o*ran)
cat —wild-cat (caht)
coille —wood (**kil**y*a*)
damh —stag (dav)
darach —oak (**dar***a*ch)
eilidh —hind (**ayl**′t^)
feadag —plover, whistler (**fed***a*k)
fraoch —heather (fröch)
gabhar —goat (**gow***a*r)
githas —pine (**gyoo′***a*s)
iolaire —eagle (yi′lara)
madadh-ruadh—fox (**mat***a*gh-**roo***a*gh)
roid —bog-myrtle (rot^)
tarmachan —ptarmigan (also Eun Fionn) (**tar***a*m*a*chan; ayn **fyoo**n)
Trilleachan —oxyster-catcher, sand-piper (tr**eel** y*a*chan)

achadh —field, often of parkland nature (**ach**agh)
airidh —sheiling (**aa′**rea)
blar —cleared space, field (blaar)
both —hut (bo)
clach —stone (klach)
dail —field, usually by water (daal^)
eas —waterfall (es)

fas — deserted place (faas)
feith — vein; sinuous stream (fe)
gort — enclosure; standing corn (gawrsht)
leis — leeward (laysh)
luib — bend, as in a stream; a little glen (**loo**eeb)
muileann — mill (**moo**l*a*n)
sneachd — snow (shnyachk)
uinneag — window (oony*a*k)

aonach — ridge (**ön**ach)
bealach — a narrow pass (b**yal**ach)
bidean — pinnacle (b**eet**y*a*n)
binnean — high, conical hill (b**een**y*a*n)
cioch — breast, breast-shaped hill (k**ee***a*ch)
ciche — genitive of cioch (k**eech***a*)
coire — cauldron (k**or***a*)
creachan — rocky surface with no vegetation, especially on a summit (k**raych***a*n)
lairig — a broad pass (l**aa**rik)
leacach — bare summit or side of a hill (lyechk*a*ch)
leathad — broad slope (lyeh*a*t)
mam — large, round hill (maam)
meall — a mound (myowl)
monadh — a range; heathy moor (mon*a*gh)
sgor and sgurr — a sharp, steep hill (skor and skoor)
sron — a nose; a promontory from a hill (srawn)
stob — a sharp point (stop)
stac — hill, steep on one side, rounded on the other (stachk).

Pronunciation

Frequently when a word takes the genitive case or the feminine gender an 'h' is inserted after the first consonant, e.g. Fuaran—fhuaran, muileann—mhuillin, mor—mhor, beag—bheag, druim—dhruim. In pronunciation mh and bh, when initial letters, sound like the English v, and fh and dh are most often aspirated. When the definite article takes the form 'an t-', it makes a following 's' silent as in Allt an-t-Sneachd—pronounced Alt an Trachka.

A useful reference work is that produced by the Royal

25

Scottish Geographical Society in 1957—A *Glossary of Gaelic and Scandinavian elements used in places names on Ordnance Survey maps.* Another is Professor W. J. Watson's *The Celtic Place Names of Scotland.* Both are out of print but should be available in a reference library.

Abbreviations, directions and terminology

Few abbreviations are used in this guide and only those in general usage. The directions left and right refer always to the direction faced by the climber, whether in ascent or descent.

Gaelic words adopted by the English language, such as cairn and bothy, are used in their English spellings unless they form part of a name, e.g. the corries of the Black Mount but Coire Chat.

SMCJ	Scottish Mountaineering Club Journal
O.S.	Ordnance Survey
m	metres
km	kilometres
ft	feet
*	Appears in chapter heading lists and indicates a 'Munro'.

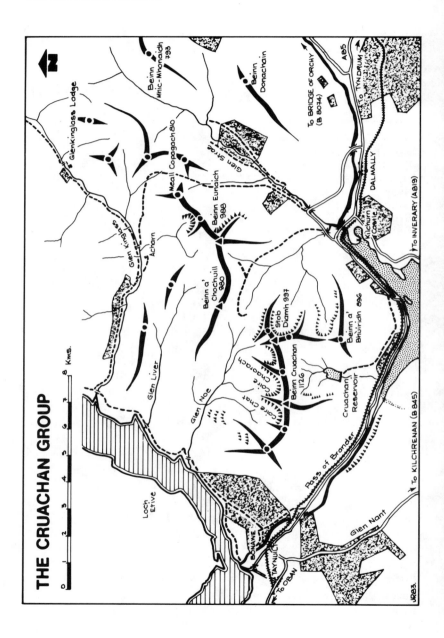

THE CRUACHAN GROUP

1

Cruachan

*Ben Cruachan (1126 m)
 Stob Dearg (1101 m)
 Meall Cuanail (916 m)
 Drochaid Ghlas (1009 m)
*Stob Diamh (997 m)
 Stob Garbh (980 m)
 Sron an Isean (964 m)
 Beinn a' Bhuiridh (896 m)

From whatever direction one approaches this splendid group, some feature of its detached and mountainous nature impresses one immediately. As a whole its extent is best seen from the south, where from some point on the eastern side of Loch Awe, the full length of its ridge can be appreciated, but it is from the north that the jagged nature of its three western tops becomes clear and indeed the view of the tops in winter from Loch Dochard, on the path between Loch Tulla and Loch Etive, is positively Alpine.

The Cruachan massif is bounded on three sides by the deep trenches of Loch Etive, the Pass of Brander and Glen Strae, while to the north the through valley of Glen Noe almost completes its isolation. A narrow ridge runs east-west for 4 km dropping below 900 m to 860 m, at one point only, and has four distinct peaks within its length, while its easternmost peak throws out ridges to the north-east and to the south, giving two more tops above 900 m. Almost to its full height the southern slopes of this range are well grassed on the granular, dioritic rock of which they are partly composed. However the ridge itself and most of the spines it throws out to the north, have an extensive exposure of granite. The acid soil supports little variety of flora but the lower, southern and western slopes carry fine woods of hazel, birch, elder, ash and small oak and the easternmost tops of the Dalmally Horsehoe produce a succulent crop of blaeberries each autumn.

Much was written about Ben Cruachan and its environs by the early travellers, though the Pass of Brander made as much impression on them as the Ben itself. In 1791 Thomas Newte rather tremulously and exaggeratedly wrote of the road through the pass as being 1000 ft up Ben Cruachan and having no parapet: that part of the old road he was describing climbed from the church west of Loch Awe village to a maximum height of 519 ft and is now under the tarmac of the road up to the Cruachan dam. Dorothy Wordsworth's sharply observed account of the journey between the heights south of Dalmally and Taynuilt is still relevant today as with the exception of the railway and the lower level road at the east end of the Pass, the general appearance of the ground can have changed little.

It needs little more than a glance at the O.S. 1:50,000 map (sheet 50) to show the attractiveness of a traverse of the main ridge and, possibly the most attractive of the possibilities, is to start up the long eastern ridge of Beinn a Bhuiridh from the western junction of the A85 with the Stronmilchan road (B8077). After the next ascent north onto the tops of the Dalmally Horseshoe, there is a switchback running west of an increasingly rugged nature terminating at Stob Dearg, Cruachan's Taynuilt Peak. If there be time left and the sky be clear, it is well worth the extra effort of descending the steep, coggly slopes west-north-west from Stob Dearg in order to be at the top of Meall nan Each for the sunset, which particularly late and early in the year can throw a path of crimson from behind the hills of Mull down the seaward length of Loch Etive. Such a traverse of course assumes either two cars in a party and a sure meeting at some point on the ridge for an exchange of keys or prior research into the use of the bus and train services between Glasgow and Oban.

Another way of traversing the tops involving return to the departure point, is that starting from the old Falls of Cruachan railway station up the path on the west side of the burn. When the dam-wall comes in sight a westerly line leads onto the broad, southern ridge of Meall Cuanail and from its top there is a mere 60 m of descent before the climb up Ben Cruachan itself.

Those who traverse north-north-west from the bealach just north of Meall Cuanail in order to reach Stob Dearg without climbing Cruachan twice, should be wary, particularly in winter, of the extensive belt of compact, red, granite slabs that lie in the way: these are best skirted by taking a low traverse line until almost below the bealach between Stob Dearg and Cruachan.

In winter the space of a full day should be allowed for the traverse. A party starting from the Falls of Cruachan will probably take 8 hours, exclusive of stops and fresh snow could add substantially to this allowance.

Beinn a' Bhuiridh (896 m)

From the east this peak has a distinctive and graceful, pyramidal shape. Its Gaelic name—Hill of the Roaring (of stags)—perhaps acrose from the reverberant properties of the enclosed coire that lies to the north of the long east ridge, though no deer will be seen there today. This latter ridge is the pleasantest approach and the initial 300 m of steep ground can be avoided by following the old railway track to the abandoned lead mine for 1 km before starting uphill to the left. The track is easily found leading north from the B8077 approximately $\frac{1}{2}$ km from Drishaig. Splendid views are to be had from this ridge, down Loch Awe and down onto Kilchurn Castle. When continuing north in winter onto the Larig Torran the descent is often icy and steep enough to require care. The Gaelic name Larig—a pass—for the saddle north of the peak, suggests that it was used as such for the black cattle grazing on the ground now occupied by the Cruachan Reservoir: it was reputed to have been used by William Wallace to outflank the men of Lorne, otherwise immovable from the narrows of the Pass of Brander. A northerly escarpment runs along the east ridge and numerous, short climbs can be enjoyed here in winter. An interesting approach to these short chimneys and gullies, takes a traverse from the Larig Torran along turf ledges which eventually run out on steep ground at one of the shallow gullies which can carry thick ice.

If this hill is included at the end of a traverse of the main ridge and descent must be made to a car left at Falls of Cruachan, the best descent is due west to the dam-head from where the path down the west side of the burn can be picked up. Descent due south to the lochside involves laborious scrambling lower down, on steep, tree-clad slopes, though one may well have one's evening toil enlivened by the hooting of tawny-owls.

Stob Diamh (997 m), Stob Garbh (980 m) and Sron an Isean (964 m)

These three peaks form an east-facing horseshoe well seen from the road east of Dalmally and better still from the Stronmilchan road. (B8077). Either of the east-south-east ridges on Sron an Isean and Stob Garbh can be approached from the old railway track mentioned under Beinn a' Bhuiridh. Bridges cross the Allt Coire Ghlais and the Allt Coire Creachain: for the first there is one close above the junction and for the latter, more than one below the junction.

Once one of the outer tops has been climbed there is only an extra 150 m of ascent and an extra kilometre involved in the circuit of all three. Both outer peaks offer some winter climbing on their eastern and northern slopes. Stob Garbh in particular throws out a north-eastern ridge from directly beneath its summit that forms a most attractive route in winter and, if the easiest line to the north of the lowest rocks is followed, is no harder than Grade I. Somewhat east of this ridge, on the northern slopes of the east-south-east ridge there is an out-crop of granite in the form of a tall slab and a buttress, that would give some hard rock-climbing. Sron an Isean's east-south-east ridge has a north face seamed with gullies and one of these, which ascends to a point on the ridge 1 km from the summit, often carries steep, though short ice-pitches in its lower half: in such conditions it would be Grade II. When making a circuit of the peaks from south to north care is needed in poor visibility at Stob Diamh since the natural trend of the ridge is due north, eventually leading in a steep and rocky descent to Glen Noe: the true east-north-east continuation is also a steep descent.

Drochaid Ghlas (1009 m) — The Grey Bridge

This fine peak set in the middle of the main ridge and often a mere incident in the course of a traverse, deserves more attention. The most repaying approach is over the Lairig Noe, from where a descending westerly traverse of 100 m and 1.5 km leads to a spur thrown down north-west from the peak's north ridge. This ridge is a narrow and exhilarating route to the summit over the occasional difficulty and over a final arête between the peak's two tops: in winter it would be classed as Grade I. Its east face is composed of very steep granite riven by vertical cracks and chimneys, while a deep gully rises to the neck between the two tops. Rock-climbs have been prospected here, but the rock is badly shattered and routes would be short.

When traversing this peak in poor visibility from either west or east the natural and almost imperceptible trend is to the north and then onto the summit which is set back north of the main ridge. The continuation of the main ridge in either direction is not well defined and a compass course will save time.

Ben Cruachan (1126 m)

All the natural routes to the summit of the main peak in the group are fittingly steep and up well defined ridges. The easiest approach is to the south ridge from the bealach north of Meall Cuanail, which can be reached by the route previously described under traverses. (Also on this side of the peak an unpleasant path ascends steeply over crumbling ground from west of and below the bealach north of Meall Cuanail. It reaches the main ridge somewhat to the east of the summit.) Then both west and east ridges involve a little scrambling, with the latter having a tricky step that requires care in winter. However, pride of place goes to the north ridge, well seen in illustration no. 5, whose aerial highway amply repays the effort of the long approach. Two ways of reaching the north ridge and the north side of the range in general are described: both involve a walk of 9 or 10 km. The first is from Bridge of Awe on the Taynuilt side of the group and uses the old, military road for 2 km before taking the private road to Glennoe Farm. A car could be taken for the initial 2 km, but permission would need to be sought for use of the private road, which is in any event very rough. Those wishing to seek permission to take a single vehicle on this dirt-road should phone Taynuilt 212. On a fine day the views from this road through the trees across Loch Etive are particularly fine.

Once the farmhouse has been skirted, the path continues up Glen Noe on the north side of the burn, which should be held up to the 200 m level in order to enjoy best the views of the northern cliffs on Stob Dearg and Cruachan and in order to pick the best line to the foot of the north ridge.

The second approach is shorter, but does involve 250 m of descent and reascent. It uses the dirt-road built during the construction of the Cruachan Dam, that reaches to a point 100 m below the Lairig Noe and commences on the B8077 on the east side of the Allt Mhoille. Curiously, the 1:50,000 First Series O.S. map (sheet 50) shows this track as discontinuous, stopping at the farm 'Castles' and recommencing at c. 380 m. Both the old 1 Inch to 1 Mile O.S. map and the current 1:25,000 (sheet NN 03/13) show the track, correctly, as continuous. The approach over the Lairig Noe offers obvious possibilities of mountaineering circuits on the northern ridges. It is also a convenient means of approaching and observing the gullies on the north face of Sron an Isean's east-south-east ridge.

Stob Dearg (1101 m)

This Gaelic name, the Red Point, for Cruachan's Taynuilt peak highlights the colour change in the granite from the grey cliffs on Drochaid Ghlas to the pink blocks that litter the west side of the Stob. If approach is being made directly to this peak, then straightforward, though laborious routes can be taken from the Pass of Brander either beside the Allt Brander or the Allt Cruiniche. A little above the railway line on either of these approaches, remnants of 'Anderson's Piano Wires' may yet be found. These were installed as an alarm system before the turn of the century, when a derailment impressed upon the railway owners the danger of falling boulders. A fence of 5659 yd length, composed of 9 ft posts carrying ten strands of steel wire, was erected through the Pass of Brander. Any boulder inflicting sufficient shock to the wires of this fence, triggered the signals and warned drivers of impending danger. The name itself originated from that of the engineer in charge of the line toward the end of the last century.

There is winter climbing on the east face of Stob Dearg of a length and quality not be found elsewhere in the range. This face has traditionally been described as the north-east face, but there is little or no 'northing' to its general inclination and those climbing there in clear weather will find the face most attractively lit by the glancing rays of the sun even at midday. The routes listed below can be reached either from the south with descent from

9. *Spindrift smoking off Ben Starav's North Ridge.* *Peter Hodgkiss*

10. *Ben Starav from Glen Etive.* *Peter Hodgkiss*

11. *A half-cantilever bridge at the junction of burns where the drainage from the great Coire na Caime joins with the lesser waters from Beinn Suidhe. Meall Garbh above Glenkinglass Lodge appears behind the bridge, and Beinn Eunaich in the distance.* Peter Hodgkiss

12. *Lower Glen Kinglass holding the remnants of oak. Site of furnace left foreground. Meall Copogach in cloud.* Peter Hodgkiss

13.   The Starav range from Màm Carraigh. The four main tops shown left to right are; Ben Starav, Glas Bheinn Mhór, Stob Coir' an Albannaich, and the dome of Meall nan Eun.

Peter Hodgkiss

14. *Glas Bheinn Mhór from the north ridge of Ben Starav.*   *Peter Hodgkiss*

15.   The Starav range from An Grianan: Beinn Trilleachan's north ridge forms a black shadow to the right; above it is Ben Starav and, moving left, Glas Bheinn Mhór, and Stob Coir' an Albannaich.
Peter Hodgkiss

16. *Stob Ghabhar from the River Bá with Sron nan Giubhas sweeping down in front.*
Peter Hodgkiss

17. *Stob Ghabhar from Loch Tulla.*   *Peter Hodgkiss*

the bealach between Stob Dearg and Cruachan itself, or the longer, but pleasanter approach, from the north through Glen Noe.

The east face makes a triangle between the south-south-east and north ridges, with its base descending toward the latter. It is composed of granite slabs steepening toward the north ridge and fissured by two, short, open gullies on its southern fringe and by two open couloirs of greater length at its centre. The first recorded ascent takes the more northerly and longer of the short gullies, while the second with its variation start, takes a line from the lowest point and close to the centre of the triangle's base.

New Year 1897 —   Grade 1
Maclay, Drummond and Parker.

The Original Route   150 m   Grade III
The north-east face of Stob Dearg is a 150 m sweep of granite slabs, bounded on one side by the north ridge. The best approach is over the col between Stob Dearg and Ben Cruachan from the Allt Brander, followed by a short easy descent to the foot of the face. Steep snow-ice covered the lowest slabs and the start was made at the bottom left-hand corner with a rising traverse to the right and then straight up. After two pitches the angle eased and straightforward climbing led to the top of the peak directly over snow.
D. J. Bennet and E. I. Thompson, April 1970.

Central Grooves   225 m   Grade IV
This route, and the following variation, are to be found on the triangular-shaped granite crag on the north-east face of the Taynuilt Peak. The crag is bounded on the right by the North Ridge and on the left by the gully of the North East Face Route, hereafter referred to as the Original Route.

In the centre of the face is a prominent groove line, rising above a short, steep corner at the top of a steep snowfield. (The snowfield may become icy grooves up granite slabs, depending on conditions). Climb the groove in three pitches to the right-hand side of a small central bay (96 m). Climb the 7 m slab corner at the top of the bay, move left into a recess, exit on the right and continue up more easily to a recess (45 m). Traverse horizontally left round an edge then up leftwards for 36 m.

35

Follow a short chimney crack to an easy groove and finish up a short overhanging chimney to belay just below the summit cairn (84 m).
I. Fulton and C. Grant, February 1978.

Original Route   60 m   Direct Start
This climbs the icefall which rises from the left-hand side of the snowfield and leads to the foot of the gully of Original Route.
C. Gilmour and C. Grant, January 1976.

All four of the northern corries have short winter climbs on their headwalls: Coire Chat has a buttress rising just east of the bealach between Stob Dearg and Cruachan that is cut by two chimneys, the westerly one being of easy angle and the easterly one vertical; Coire Caorach has some gully lines on the north-westerly aspect of Drochaid Ghlas, as has the nameless corrie to the east at the north-east angle between Drochaid Ghlas and the main ridge; and the hanging corrie—Coire Lochain—presents steep ground, often icy, to the summit of Stob Diamh.

Meall Cuanail (916 m)

This southern spur of Cruachan itself is a modest lump in very grand surroundings and is usually ascended on the way to the main peak by the route from the Falls of Cruachan.

Where to Stay

There are hotels and guest-houses at both Dalmally and Taynuilt, while at Bridge of Awe there is a guest-house with a caravan and camp-site at the one place. At Lochawe, the Holiday Fellowship now own the hotel so magnificently situated on a promontory above Loch Awe.

References

SMCJ, II, p. 85. For a thrilling account by W. Douglas of the first ascent of Stob Dearg's north ridge under unusually icy conditions (1882).
A Progress in Mountaineering, J. H. B. Bell, p. 8. For another account of a winter ascent of Stob Dearg's north ridge (1936).

SMCJ, XI, p. 236. Loch Awe in the time of Bruce and Wallace. An interesting
  introduction to the history of the warfare waged through the Pass of
  Brander.

SMCJ, XII, pp. 65, 137 and 189. These articles of antiquarian interest about the
  islands of Loch Awe.

Prospects and Observations on a Tour of England and Scotland. Thomas Newte
  (1791).

A Tour in Scotland: 1803. Dorothy Wordsworth (James Thin, Edinburgh,
  1974).

Expostulation with Cruachan

Of Crechanben the crewilte,
The driftis dreich, the hichtis hie,
It sair wald tene my tong to tell;
Quha suld reherss thy painis fell
Forgaitheris with the frenesie

With fensom feiris thou art forfairn,
Ay yowland lyk ane busteous bairn;
With mauchie mistis thy mirth is marrit,
With skowland skyis thy spreit is skarrit,
And seitis ar cauld upon thy cairn.

Quhair is thy lown illuminat air,
Thy fre fassoun, thy foirheid fair?
Quhair is thy peirles pulchritude?
Quhy stayis thou nocht as anis thou stude?
Quhy girnis and greitis thou evirmair?

Return agane fra drowpand dule!
Restoir thy pure wayfarand fule,
And lat him se thee quhair thou smylis,
With Mul, Arane, and the Owt-Ylis,
Into the lufsom licht of Yule

W. P. Ker

2

The Glen Strae Hills

*Beinn a' Chochuill (980 m)
*Beinn Eunaich (989 m)
 Beinn Mhic Mhonaidh (793 m)

This scattered group of hills are bounded to the east and south by Glen Orchy and Glen Noe and to the north by Glen Kinglass and by the path from the head of the latter glen to Victoria Bridge. A mail-bus service between Bridge of Orchy and Dalmally makes possible the long walk up Glen Strae and over the tops to Bridge of Orchy, but the extensive afforestation on the western slopes of Glen Orchy curtails approach from this side.

One natural traverse over the big hills presents itself, with a convenient approach via the hydro-road leading onto the southern slopes of Beinn a' Chochuill and with the day's end on the track down the lower part of Glen Strae after a descent from Beinn Larachan.

Beinn a' Chochuill (980 m)

Though dwarfed and hidden by its splendid neighbour Ben Cruachan, this hill does have a distinctive form being an elongated ridge running east to west. Indeed a traverse from Loch Etive to the Lairig Lanachain involves a distance of 9 km. Such a roundabout approach will rarely be undertaken, but anyone climbing from Loch Etive is recommended to include A' Chruach (271 m) behind Glennoe farm, for the magnificent view both up and down the Loch. The obvious approach is via the Hydro-Board track from Castles Farm, described earlier in Chapter 1. After crossing the main burn descending from the bealach between Beinn a' Chochuill and Beinn Eunaich, the track should be left for the easy ascent of the south-easterly ridge that descends from Point 896 m—an easterly fore-top and one of many on the 1 km ridge to the summit. Once on the ridge the splendour of the view towards Cruachan's three westerly peaks becomes apparent and improves until it is at its best a little beyond the summit. So splendid is this view that it would almost be worthwhile to climb the north face of Beinn a' Chochuill in order to enjoy the breathtaking impact of it as one's head popped over the cornice. For this superb composition of ridge, corrie and peak to be enjoyed at its best, ascent before midday on a clear winter's day is recommended.

Though it provides no recognised winter climbs, the north face is continuously steep throughout its 3 km breadth and care is needed on the ridge which often carries a large and continuous cornice. The ground to the north around the head of Glen Liver is a desolation of peat-bog, moraines and lochans, but has a real sense of remoteness and is as likely a place as any on the east side of Loch Etive from which to see eagles soaring and swooping, or even to spot fox and wild-cat with the aid of binoculars.

Beinn Eunaich (989 m)

Though joined to Beinn a' Chochuill at the Lairig Lanachain (728 m), Beinn Eunaich has a somewhat different form. This is partially due to the band of porphyry that outcrops on a north-eastern shoulder of Beinn Eunaich and interrupts the granite of which the two hills are mainly composed, but also Beinn Eunaich has a more pyramidal shape, radiating three ridges and holding a fine corrie to the east. The ascent can be made straightforwardly from Castles Farm, over steep ground to the fore-peak Stob Maol and then along the broad, easy-angled south ridge, but this ridge is pleasanter in descent for the fine views it gives of Loch Awe and of the long ridges of the 'Dalmally Horseshoe'. A more interesting route will be found on the opposite side of the mountain.

Starting up the track on the west of the River Strae and keeping left at the fork, a patch of afforestation is reached in 1 km. From its northern rim a faint path follows the west bank of the main burn (unnamed on the 1:50,000 O.S. map) that drains the cirque formed by Beinn Eunaich, Meall Copogach and Beinn Lurachan. (This path, the depiction of which on various maps, has been the subject of raillery for the past 90 years—William Douglas, *SMCJ*, Vol. II—is still shown confidently on the 1:50,000 O.S. First Series. It certainly comes and goes and should not be relied upon north of the bealach). In a little over 30 minutes, the 'Black Shoot' and its containing buttress of porphyry will be seen steeply above to the left and in a further 30 minutes the foot of a ridge running down east from the unnamed top (880 m) will be reached. This, and then Beinn Eunaich's steep north-east ridge, give an approach of greater interest.

At one time Beinn Eunaich was best known for its 'Black Shoot' and a train of aspirants attacked it, and were usually repulsed, in the years about the end of the last century. There are no fewer than 21 references to it in the first 8 volumes of the SMC Journal and any modern climber contemplating an ascent could prepare himself by reading accounts by two of these ancients and one by a modern whose wit is well seasoned with awe: The Black Shoot of Stob Maol, W. R. Lester, *SMCJ*, Vol. II, p. 117; The Black Shoot in White, H. Raeburn, *SMCJ*, Vol. VI, p. 161; Pink Elephants in the Black Shoot, R. N. Campbell, *SMCJ*, XXX, p. 21. The climb is up a series of chimneys, well vegetated and seemingly always wet. It is at least Severe in standard.

The hill is also revered as the place where that most generous and far-sighted spirit Percy Unna crossed the Great Divide. Warned off the hill by his doctor because of a serious heart condition, Unna preferred to continue his hill wandering but out of consideration for others chose to go alone. He did not return from one of his solitary walks and was found dead on the slopes below Stob Maol. A man of great wealth Unna chose to disperse much of it toward the purchase of mountain land for the use of hill-goers and, using the National Trust as a vehicle for anonymous donations, was instrumental in the purchase of mountainous areas such as Glencoe and Kintail.

Meall Copogach (810 m), Beinn Lurachan (715 m)

A traverse of Beinn a' Chochuill and Beinn Eunaich extends quite naturally over these two tops and Beinn Lurachan's south-west ridge is well drained and easy going for descent. Rough slabs of pink granite crop out lower down and, at its foot above a new bridge on the Glen Strae track, there is a magnificent swimming-pool. For those walking from Dalmally to Bridge of Orchy, Beinn Lurachan is a good point at which to take to the hills since Glen Strae narrows considerably beyond it and the view becomes restricted. A rather tenuous line can then be followed over **Beinn Larachan** (586 m) and on to **Beinn Suidhe** (675 m). This walk gives ever-changing views of the Ben Starav and Black Mount Hills and of their deeply recessed glens. It ends in a fine situation as one descends Beinn Suidhe's north-east ridge toward an isolated stand of firs beside a confluence of burns.

Beinn Mhic Mhonaidh (793 m)

From Glen Strae this hill looks every inch a mountain, presenting as it does a classical cone shape with steep sides. It is not easy of access, for the Strae can be difficult to ford opposite the foot of the south-west ridge. There is a bridge (O.S. NN166315) in the second patch of afforestation which crosses east to the old path up the glen and eventually to the shieling of Inbhir-nan-giubhas, but no one should be tempted here as the old path is now very rough going through densely packed spruce. (This corner is worth visiting though on an off-day for the delightful series of waterfalls and for the remnants of Scots Pine that mingle with the new firs and appear majestic by contrast.)

When the river is full the first place at which it can be forded is where the track itself crosses over to the east bank (O.S. NN186338) and even then care will be needed. The slopes above are steep, riven with drainage channels, and higher, of scree; and the alternative of trending diagonally right (south) to gain the south-west ridge is recommended. Descent from Beinn Mhic Mhonaidh to Glen Orchy is not advised as a way must be found through the extensive afforestation.

To continue over Beinn Mhic Mhonaidh and on to Bridge of Orchy involves some rough going at the head of Glen Strae and at the double-level bealach between Beinn Mhic Mhonaidh, **Beinn a'Churn** (564 m) and **Meall an Laoigh** (546 m), where also the terrain can be confusing in poor visibility. Intervening ridges prevent the fine views that are enjoyed from the previously mentioned traverse, but this route is the quicker, avoiding the

9 km walk from Clashgour to Bridge of Orchy and once **Ben Inverveigh**'s long ridge has been traversed northward, an excellent track leads down directly to Bridge of Orchy from the Mam Carraigh. The temptation to descend due west from Beinn Inverveigh's northernmost top, should be resisted as the struggle through the forest will absorb any time saved.

For anyone staying in the vicinity of Loch Tulla, a walk up Beinn Inverveigh on a clear evening will be amply repaid, as the westering sun highlights the ridges and models the corries of the Starav and Black Mount groups to great effect. The view of the north-west quadrant is fine enough from the Mam Carraigh, but as one gradually gains height on a good track, the panorama extends until it includes an arc from Beinn nan Aighenan to Clach Leathad and Beinn Toaig. From the Mam Carraigh one can also look down on the old enclosures and the more recent wood above the Allt Tologhan, that marks the area of the croft in which the Gaelic poet, Duncan Ban McIntyre, was born. Even though his poetry is said not to translate with its full effect into English—losing the cadence of Gaelic and it's changing rhythm, as of the piobaireachd, that Duncan Ban used deliberately—his poems, and one 'Beinn Dorain', transmit a sense of elan at approaching a hill and an appreciation of landscape that will strike a chord with most hill-goers.

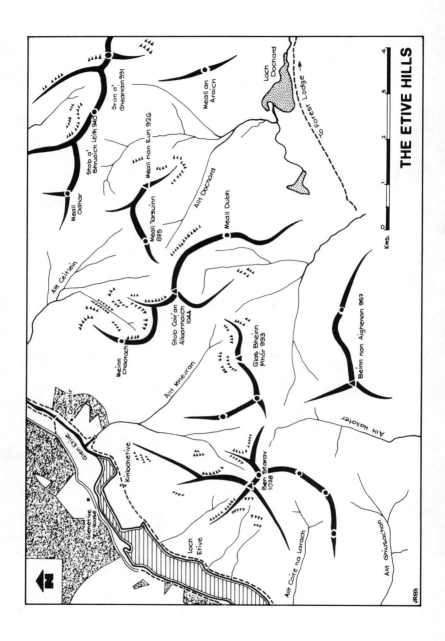

THE ETIVE HILLS

3

Ben Starav Group

*Ben Starav (1078 m)
*Stob Coir' an Albannaich (1044 m)
*Beinn nan Aighenan (957 m)
*Glas Bheinn Mhór (993 m)
*Meall nan Eun (926 m)

This group of hills is clearly bounded to the west and to the south by Loch Etive and Glen Kinglas and, a little less clearly to the north and to the east by the Allt Ceitlin and Allt Dochard, with the scatter of lochans below the latter burn completing the eastern boundary. The hills are characterised by deeply recessed glens and by large exposures of the creamy and rough Etive granite, sometimes in extensive pavements on the high ridges, sometimes in vast slabs spilling down from the bealachs and making idyllic, summer highways in the beds of the major burns. All the tops are most conveniently reached from Glen Etive, but starting from Victoria Bridge does allow a more open view. Though at a great distance from the nearest road, there are some extensive catchment-areas of snow for those who enjoy ski-ing away from the crowds.

Ben Starav (1078 m)

From Glen Etive this hill stands up proudly above the head of the loch, looking its full height and of an appearance agreeing with the derivation of its name suggested by some Gaelic speakers, i.e. an abbreviation from Starbhanach meaning a stout, bulky man with a small head. The most straightforward ascent is up the well-defined, north ridge, reached by crossing the bridge a little north of Coileitir and then following the path to a second bridge crossing this time the Allt Mheuran. Both these bridges occupy fine situations; the first looking down on a pool of great depth shadowed by deciduous trees; and the second spanning a burn lined with a delightful variety of trees—Scots Pine, holly, birch—and looking up to a series of short waterfalls dropping green into creamy granite basins. When crossing the bridge at Coileitir, it is an arresting thought that in the winter of 1906, it was immersed in a flash-flood—a rise of at least 7 m. The north ridge sweeps up with just one relatively level section at mid-height and with an escarpment on its eastern rim, directly to the summit cairn.

There are three tops to Beinn Starav, a second (1068 m) lying to the south-east, and a third (Stob Coire Dheirg, 1020 m) reached from the second by an arête of shattered quartzite and granite running east-north-east. On the flanks of this arête where the granite has eroded into gravel, can be found the cushions of moss-campion-flowering from June on. Stob Coire Dheirg is the culminating point of a fine corrie, Coire Dearg, buttressed with crazy turrets of shattered granite, but also containing some gullies which with their north-easterly aspect and, commencing at such great height, offer good winter climbing. None is more serious than Grade II and none gives more than 100 m of ascent. Coire Dearg is best reached by an excellent stalker's path which follows the west side of the burn forking south-south-west at O.S. 140451 (Allt nan Meirleach). Another approach to Ben Starav is extremely long, involving a round trip of c. 42 km from Victoria Bridge. However for those walking across country, or able to organise cars at Victoria Bridge and Glen Etive, this long walk from the east carries one beside the chuckle of the Linne nam Beathach, broad and shallow for a burn of comparable drainage; over a watershed almost imperceptible in Highland terms, where two burns falling east from Beinn Suidhe and not 100 m apart diverge to flow to either side of the watershed; and into the recesses of the great Coire na Caime where lies the source of the River Kinglass which here falls in a series of waterfalls, ravines and pools ideal for swimming and where numerous rickles of stone speak of summer shielings.

Those following this route in reverse and in poor visibility will need to exercise care with compass readings at the bealach between Ben Starav and the unnamed top to the east, as also at the lower bealach below Bein nan Aighenan's north ridge.

There are exposures of granite slabs at high angle on Ben

Starav's west-facing slopes at c. 400 m above Kinlochetive. They are more featureless and more affected by drainage than the famous Etive Slabs across the Loch. Though again not offering the same vertical length of route as the latter slabs, they offer a taste of exploration for those climbing comfortably at the Very Severe level.

Stob Coir' an Albannaich (1044 m)

With its satellite Beinn Chaorach (850 m) this hill extends 9 km from south-east to north-west. To its north a narrow spur falls between gorges into Glen Ceitlein and to the south an even narrower spur drops from Sron na h'Iolaire (510 m) to the watershed above Loch Dochard. Both spurs make fine routes to the summit with the former adding zest to a winter ascent and the latter perhaps better appreciated without snow.

When leaving the path approximately 9 km out from Victoria Bridge, the driest ground beneath Sron na h'Iolaire will be found just to the south of Lochan na h'Iuraiche, from where the ridge is soon gained. From the ridge one's eye follows the glen over Lochs Dochard and Tulla in an uninterrupted view to the drainage-furrowed flanks of Beinn Achaladair and higher there is an expanse of granite slabs on Meall Dubh at an angle and of a roughness that is a delight to walk up. The summit sports an unusually large cairn—a relic of early theodolite triangulation by the Ordnance Survey. From Glen Etive one starts, as with all the hills in this group, at the bridge above Coileitir. The apparent bridge shown 1 km to the north on both the current 1:50,000 O.S. map and the old One Inch to One Mile O.S. map (but without the significant letters FB) is in fact a pulley bridge, i.e. a gondola suspended from wires, not intended for public use.

A good track runs north from Coileitir and then east for a short distance up Glen Ceitlein, which rises little for 2 km when, the two gorges with their birch remnants come into view. The steep, northern spur is bedecked with blocks of granite and needs a little care in icy conditions, but the ground falls away more steeply on either side where the granite blocks seem even more crazily perched.

Both the northern and main tops are fronted to the north-east by crags, that under the main summit being a sweep of very steep granite, unfortunately too short for worthwhile climbing.

47

If it is intended to continue on to Meall Tarsuinn (875 m) care should be taken in poor visibility as a dog-leg movement first due east then back west of north is needed. Care is also advised in winter as the slope is steep, rocky and often icy.

A compass bearing is again worthwhile when descending south-west in poor visibility perhaps to continue over Glas Bheinn Mhor, as the natural trend of the ground leads out onto a south-easterly spur. This south-westerly aspect of Stob Coir' an Albannaich is noted for its snow collecting properties.

Beinn Chaorach (the hill of the sheep, known locally in Glen Etive as Stob Leitir) is notable for its consistent steepness on all sides and whilst a way can be picked down the hillside above Glen Etive, it is steep and is pocked with granite slabs usually wet with seepage—no place to descend on a winter's evening. These same outcroppings of granite occur over much of the summit area and granite appears again in steep ribs with a slabby apron on the slope dropping into the gorge east of the summit area. Routes have been made here and the following descriptions are taken from the SMC Journal.

A well-defined area of cracks and deep V-grooves divides the crag into two portions: to the left of these faults is an expanse of steep slabs, to the right are three narrow buttresses. The leftmost buttress has a striking pink slab, capped by a line of overhangs. The two routes reported lie on this buttress. The rock is sound and nowhere difficult.

Central Rib   120 m   Difficult
Takes the line of least resistance up the buttress, finishing up the rib bounding the prominent pink slab on the right.
J. R. Marshall and R. N. Campbell, April 1967.

Eazay Edge   105 m   Severe
Follows the left edge of the buttress throughout.
J. Brumfitt and B. Sproul, May 1967.

Patey's Old Man   20 m   Unclassifiable
This striking pinnacle protrudes from the left wall of the gorge. Lasso the top and climb the rope. Treat it gently.
I. Rowe and B. Sproul, May 1967.

Xenolith   140 m   Very Severe

At the right of the crag and at three-quarter height is a prominent black overlap. The following route climbs the slabby rib leading directly to the right end of the overlap. Above the lowest rocks is a small, curving overlap. Start 7 m left at a small cairn. Climb slabs to steep rib, move up then left to small stance at pink rocks (60 m). Climb steep slab past large block and follow system of quartz veins to enter obvious rectangular recess. Step left and move up flake belay (32 m). Climb groove then thin crack at right end of large overlap and continue up carious slabs to peg belay just below grass ledge (45 m). Finish by a choice of routes up short walls, better to left (33 m).

K. V. Crocket and Miss K. Simpson, July 1972.

Deadline   140 m   Severe

Start 7 m left of Xenolith at large boulder. The route climbs fairly directly up always on the left of a natural watercourse to the left end of the black overlap mentioned in the description of Xenolith.

K. V. Crocket and C. Stead, July 1972.

Beinn nan Aighenan (957 m)

One of the more remote hills in the Central Highlands, Beinn nan Aighenan is moated on all sides by the waters of the Kinglass and the Allt Hallater, above which rise steep and grassy slopes—stirring admiration for the black cattle who perhaps roamed these slopes—the Gaelic name means hill of the heifers. The only break in these defences occurs in a small area to the north where a ridge drops to a bealach that itself must be reached by crossing another—that between Ben Starav and the top to its east (unnamed on the O.S. 1:50,000 map: Meall nan Tri Tighearnan on the O.S. 1:25,000 map). When using this approach from Coileitir in Glen Etive, interest is added by climbing the long, low spur thrown out north by the latter top: it gives fine views into Ben Starav's Coire Dearg and a distinctive view rearward to the Bealach Fhionnghaill, in front of which a series of bisecting ridges lends an impression of telescoping.

A second approach is that using the path from Victoria Bridge. Once over the watershed beyond Loch Dochard a descent of 100 m and 1.5 km leads to a half-cantilever bridge at a

49

junction of burns. Above a very steep slope of 350 m eases onto a splendid ridge undulating and twisting for 3 km over exposures of rough, cream-coloured granite. The last route described is perhaps too lengthy to be used in anything but a crossing of the hills: it uses the faint path over the bealach between Meall Copogach and Beinn Lurachan, following the main burn down to a junction, with birch remnants about a waterfall, when a crossing should be made for a traverse to the foot-bridge over the Kinglass at O.S. 153368. From here the track leads north to the Allt Hallater which descends through a wooded gorge. A good stalker's path follows the north-east side of the burn (immediately above to the north is a ravine with some short rock-pitches) and should be held until it climbs temporarily from the burn, when ascent north from this point leads to a plateau at c. 700 m and then to the south-south-west spur of Beinn nan Aighenan. Despite the long and in places, rough approach, the scenery in the lower reaches of the Allt Hallater and the remoteness of its setting, make the effort well worthwhile.

The higher reaches of the Allt Hallater gather large accumulations of snow in most winters and would provide good runs for those seeking to ski in solitude.

Ben nan Lus (709 m) and Stob an Duine Ruaidh (800 m)

For those walking up the east-side of Loch Etive and intending to include an ascent of Ben Starav, an approach across these two small hills will add interest. Armaddy and the spur behind it are an obvious starting point for the first hill, but a glance at the O.S. map would not prepare one for the extent of the plateau above with its scattered multitude of tiny lochans. At the foot of the hill's northerly spur is another tiny lochan, not more than 100 m from the Allt Hallater, but which drains in the opposite direction towards Loch Etive. Few might consider descending the 100 m or so from Starav's southerly ridge to sit for a while on Stob an Duine Ruaidh, but the view will compensate for the lost height, there being a lack of intervening ground to interrupt the splendour of Cruachan's northern ridges, added to which the steep slopes beneath to west and south give a sense of isolation above the loch.

18. Bá Bridge.   Peter Hodgkiss

19.   Stob a' Choire Odhair and Beinn Toaig from the summit of the Black Mount.

Peter Hodgkiss

20.   *Walking off Clach Leathad's easterly nose—Sron nam Forsair—down to Bá Bridge.*
Peter Hodgkiss

21.   *In amongst the great glens to the north of Stob Ghabhar. Taken from low on Aonach Mór with the sun-lit ridge of Sŕon a' Ghearrain—rising to the centre.*   *Bert Jenkins*

22. *Descending toward the Bealach Fuar-chathaidh above the Allt Ghiubhasan.*

Peter Hodgkiss

23.   Sron na Creise.   *Peter Hodgkiss*

24.   *Looking up Glen Etive from An Grianan with Stob Dubh right of centre, cleft by its gorge.*   *Peter Hodgkiss*

25.   The fine waterfall just below the point where the Allt Coire Odhair joins the Allt Coire Ghiubhasan.   Peter Hodgkiss

26.   *Clach Leathad from the River Bá.*   *Peter Hodgkiss*

Glas Bheinn Mhór (993 m)

Either of the approaches from Glen Etive or from Victoria Bridge described under Ben Starav and Beinn nan Aighenan apply equally to this hill, which presents a pleasantly symmetrical profile when seen from the road about Druimachoish. Descent from the bealach east-north-east is wet going, but leads to the 'Robbers' Waterfall' on the Allt Mheuran, which is a spectacular fall. Ascent or descent of Glas Bheinn Mhór on its northern slopes involves tiresomely, steep ground well worth avoiding.

Meall nan Eun (926 m)

Though accurately described by Gaels as a 'round shaped hill' (of the bird), Meall nan Eun has been unfairly dismissed as dull and uninteresting. No hill in this group is composed of such consistently steep ground, with only a northern ridge presenting straightforward routes. Through an arc from north-north-east to south-west the flat top is surrounded by slopes that fall away uncompromisingly and the whole of the north-eastern slope is interrupted by plaques of granite set at a high angle. Ascent by dint of a little scrambling can be made at any point in this arc, but for descent open slopes will be found only in the south western corner.

The pleasantest approach from Victoria Bridge is to follow the stalker's path (unmarked on the O.S. 1:50,000) that climbs north-west from Clashgour over the bealach between Meall an Araich and Stob Ghabhar. When the path fades, a descending traverse to the Allt Dochard allows a scramble on the rough granite in the bed of the basin until the bealach is reached on the north of the hill. If returning to Victoria Bridge, the ground about Loch Dochard should be avoided—it is a waste of bog, tussocks and hidden pools, while skirting the loch on the west in order to reach the path involves fording deep burns.

From Glen Etive the river, when low, can be forded at a point just north of the pulley bridge at Glenceitlin and the glen then followed to the bealach on the north of Meall nan Eun.

Study of the O.S. map (Sheet 50) shows the feasability, even on a winter's day, of traversing all the hills in this group that

C

front onto Glen Etive, though inclusion of Beinn nan Aighenan makes for a tall order and is in any event somewhat artificial. On a clear day without fresh snow to hinder one, this circuit from Coileitir is thoroughly recommended.

Glen Kinglass and Loch Etive

Outside that summer period from July to early September when the midge can make low-level walking a penitential exercise, the walk between Bridge of Orchy and Taynuilt provides fine contrast between the barren stretch of high moorland east of the Loch Dochard watershed and the lush, deciduous woodlands in the narrow Glen Kinglass. To the east of the watershed the Linne nam Beathach flows broad and shallow over a bed of pink granite shingle and boulders and to the west the Kinglass spills over great saucers of grey granite, which under strong sunlight can heat the water almost to body-temperature. Bird-life abounds in lower Glen Kinglass and on Loch Etive side, where also seals can often be seen basking on the islets off the point of Inverliver Bay. The shore line at Inverliver also has interest in the spring that wells out of the shingle and is known to have been there for the last 50 years: though the loch is salt to the taste at this point its margins freeze in hard winters, when the spring leaves a clear track in the ice as it flows into the loch.

In the lower reaches of Glen Kinglass, the remains of old furnaces and charcoal beds can be found here and there and oak, hazel and birch still grow strongly. Though the full distance of approximately 45 km makes a good step in a day, there is an excellent track. Those planning to take two days over this walk would need to carry a tent as there are no recognised bothies en route.

Another low-level walk of interest is that from Taynuilt to the head of Loch Etive and here the boat plying in summer between Auchnacloich and the head of Loch Etive should be borne in mind (see Introduction, p. 2). Half-way up the loch, Armaddy, once renowned as the granary of Glen Etive, occupies the site of a fluvial outflow and the rich silt provides good pasture-land.

Further north a low wall is all that remains of the church by the Allt Ghiusachan—evidence of the scattered community of the loch side and Glen Kinglass in previous centuries. This latter burn together with the Allt Coire na Larach and that draining the north-north-west corrie of Ben Starav, are difficult to cross after heavy rain.

Accommodation

See Chapters 1 and 4.

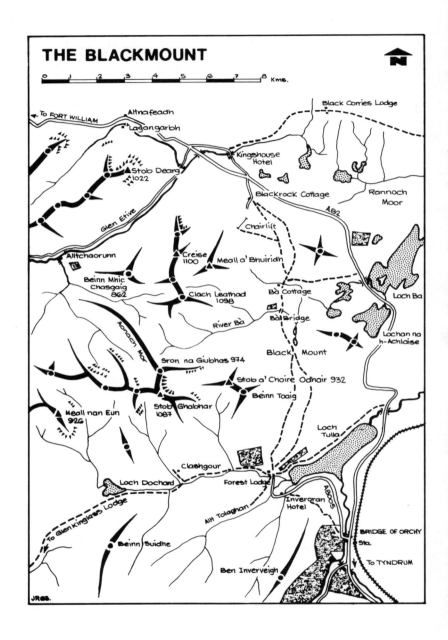

THE BLACKMOUNT

0 1 2 3 4 5 6 7 8 Kms.

To FORT WILLIAM

Altnafeadh

Lagangarbh

Kingshouse Hotel

Black Corries Lodge

Stob Dearg 1022

Glen Etive

Blackrock Cottage

A82

Rannoch Moor

Alltchaorunn

Creise 1100

Meall a' Bhuiridh

Chairlift

Beinn Mhic Chasgaig 862

Clach Leathad 1098

Bà Cottage

Loch Ba

Aonach Mor

River Bà

Bà Bridge

Lochan na h-Achlaise

Sron na Giubhas 974

Black Mount

Stob a' Choire Odhair 932

Beinn Toaig

Meall nan Eun 926

Stob Ghabhar 1087

Loch Tulla

Clashgour

Loch Dochard

Forest Lodge

A8005

Invergran Hotel

To Glen Kinglass Lodge

Allt Tolaghan

BRIDGE OF ORCHY Sta.

To TYNDRUM

Beinn Suidhe

Ben Inverveigh

JR88.

4

The Black Mount

Stob Ghabhar (1087 m)
Stob a' Bhruaich Léith (940 m)
Stob Dubh, Beinn Ceitlein (883 m)
Stob a' Choire Odhar (932 m)
Clach Leathad (1098 m)
Stob a' Ghlais Choire (996 m)
Creise (1100 m)
Meall a' Bhuiridh (1108 m)

The best features of this magnificent group of hills are hidden from roadside view. It is only from the old road, in the vicinity of Bà Bridge, that one can begin to appreciate the splendour of Coireach a' Bà and its sister, Coire Dhearbhadh, while from Glen Etive it is impossible to look into the twin defiles that drain Aonach Mor. More than any group of hills in the Central Highlands, other than perhaps those of the Corrour Forest, is this the province of the red deer. It is also of interest for the complexity of its geology which though mainly of Cruachan Granite is interrupted by mica-schist, quartzite and gneiss—a junction of gneiss and Cruachan granite crossing close to the top of Stob Ghabhar.

Stob Ghabhar (1087 m)

For complexity of form and for the splendour of its corries and glens, this hill has few equals in the Central Highlands. It throws out a series of roughly parallel ridges to the north-west and two others to the east that enclose a fine hanging corrie: only to the south does it present relatively gentle slopes. Victoria Bridge beside Loch Tulla is the obvious starting point and also offers the shortest route to the summit. A stalker's path, not marked on sheet 50 of O.S. 1:50,000 First Series, strikes north beside the Allt Toaig from the old schoolhouse, which is now run as a club-hut by the Glasgow University Mountaineering Club. (This corrugated metal tower is reputed to sleep 12 people, which reputation will be a source of wonder to all who walk past). The path on the east side of the burn runs out perhaps ½ km short of the bealach between Stob Ghabhar and Stob a' Choire Odhar, but it is worth continuing to the bealach for the view on the other side of the glacier-scarred corrie with its lip dropping sharply toward the lower Coire Dhearbhadh. From the bealach a scramble over rough ground leads to the east-south-east ridge, Aonach Eagach, with the view of the cliff enclosing the Upper Couloir providing ample excuse for halts on the coggly slopes. Once on the ridge there is a splendid highway to the top, narrowing in places to an arête that requires care under icy conditions. The east-south-east ridge can be gained more directly by crossing the Allt Toaig from about the point where the path runs out: at its south-eastern extremity there is a small crag of granite on which climbs of Very Difficult to Severe standard have been made. The climbing is delicate and not over-generous in holds and the maximum height is 30 m. More entertainment can be found at the left-hand side of the crag where the bed of the water-fall has been climbed after a spell of dry weather.

Return from the top offers choice for all tastes. Most direct is the route down the south-south-east spur running off the Aonach Eagach but sections of this spur are tiresomely steep and a traverse of 1 km west to the top above Sron a' Ghearrain (980 m) then offers easy-angled slopes down to the belach north of **Meall an Araich** (685 m), where a stalker's path leads down to Clashgour (Neil Munro in 'The New Road' has Campbell and MacMaster using this track in their crossing to Glen Etive). However more repaying by far is the circuit of the eastern, hanging corrie, travelling initially north and soon crossing the junction of gneiss and granite, made obvious by the transition from short grass to a boulder-field of pink and grey granite, then trending right and east to descend over the sharp spine of **Sron nan Guibhas** (The Nose of the Firs: pronounced Geevas) with the prospect of Rannoch Moor widening before one and the slopes on either side dropping steeply into glaciated corries. If a party has the intention of continuing to Bà Bridge and returning by the old road, then the north side of the River Bà should be gained directly from the foot of the Sron nan Guibhas. The river cannot be forded easily further downstream and there is a track on only the north side. A line taken directly east from Sron nan Guibhas crosses poorly drained ground that can be very wet indeed.

The two approaches from Glen Etive involve greater distances but both have interest and that over Aonach Mór has a unique scenic quality. To reach Aonach Mór's north-western toe one has first to surmount the gate of corrugated metal on the Alltchaorunn bridge where combined tactics may be needed. Once past the disused shooting lodge keep to the path, worn through to the granite, on the east side of the Allt a' Chaoruinn for 1 km to a junction where the burn must be crossed. This burn has cut a spectacular channel in its granite bed and falls into a series of pools culminating in very deep water beneath the bridge just above the lodge. Roughly 1 km upstream from the lodge there is a square-cut cleft known locally as Fraser's Leap, from the feat performed by one of the Marquess of Breadalbane's stalkers.

There is a steep pull of perhaps 200 m before the ridge begins to level out, but there is a splendid, high-level walk of 5 km to the summit. In thick weather the trend of the ground carries one out onto Sron nan Giubhas and a compass bearing will save time. Those with time to spare and the thirst to justify a search might turn aside and a little downhill before the final slope of Stob Ghabhar to hunt for the spring near the head of the Allt Coire a' Chaolain (at NN228459). The second approach from Glen Etive uses the route up Glen Ceitlin described in the previous chapter under Stob Coir' an Albannaich. Once past the twin gorges with their birch remnants, that lie on the northern flanks of Stob Coir' an Albannaich a steep nose leads up in approximately 250 m to Meall Odhar (876 m) from where a ridge twists and undulates over Sron a' Ghearrain (980 m) to the top. If this route is being used for descent in poor visibility the line of the fence of old iron stobs follows that of the parish boundary only so far as Sron a' Ghearrain where, it swings away to the south. As a route to the top of Stob Ghabhar it has most to commend it as one leg of a circuit over Stob Ghabhar and the Starav group.

For parties crossing the hills, or with transport to Victoria

Bridge and from Glen Etive, and wanting to avoid the tops in poor weather the following makes a fine walk through a great variety of scenery. Take the stalker's path from Clashgour to the bealach north of Meall an Araich, drop then to follow the Allt Dochard to the bealach north of Meall nan Eun, from where drop again before trending north to cross the last bealach between Meall Odhar and Beinn Ceitlein to follow the Allt a' Chaoruinn, with a path on its west bank, down to the bridge at the shooting lodge. This stravaig has more mountain flavour to it than many a hill-walk and here and there in the middle section one can find traces of the path evidencing century-long use of such routes through the hills. It would be unusual not to see during such a day one of the large herds of deer that graze these slopes.

There is climbing of a general mountaineering nature on three sides of Stob Ghabhar: it is all satisfyingly remote with the only likelihood of meeting another party being in the Upper Couloir. In the deep-cut corrie—Coire Ghabhar—lying to the east, there is a winter route that takes the 100 m gully cleaving the head-wall and finishing steeply not 50 m east of a point 980 m above Sron a' Ghearrain. This route often carries steep ice in its lower half and is therefore Grade II. Almost directly below the summit and facing a little north of east lies the buttress cloven by the Upper Couloir. This climb occupies a place in the early annals of winter climbing on a par with Tower Ridge and the Black Shoot of Beinn Eunaich. Successive waves of SMC parties attacked the route as impressed by its surroundings as by the difficulties of the climbing. The first complete ascent took place in 1897 when A. E. Mayland led Professor Adamson, Mrs. Adamson and Miss Weiss. Most of these early parties made the Lower Couloir part of their approach, but this involves a leftward traverse to reach the foot of the Upper Couloir across a snow-slope very prone to avalanche. It is certainly quicker to ascend the broad gully that drops from the neck between Aonach Eagach and Stob Ghabhar and to make a rightward traverse above more open slopes. If there be deep snow in the corrie, it will be quicker still to traverse the Aonach Eagach to the neck and descend the broad gully. In thick weather the narrow entrance to the Upper Couloir is not easily found.

Particularly in early winter, before snow-fall has banked-out the lower-pitch and shortened the frozen waterfall above, the route can be very difficult and fully deserving a Grade III category. Other routes on the buttress split by the Upper Couloir are as follows:

Hircine Rib   110 m   Severe
Start at the foot of the lowest rocks on the left of the Upper Couloir. Climb slightly leftward on steepening rock to an awkward, sloping ledge at 28 m. Above is an undercut and friable rib with a steep, smooth groove to its left. Climb the groove and easier rocks above to belay at 37 m. A further section of 20 m starting with an airy corner leads to easy ground and scrambling for the last 60 m to the summit ridge. The rock is a compact quartz-felspar, riven into vertical furrows and with mainly out-sloping holds. It is loose in places and lacking in belays.
P. Mitchell, J. Morrison and J. R. Ewing, 21st May 1961.

Capricorn   65 m   Grade III
Climb the rib bounding the right side of the Upper Couloir leading to a knife-edge arête culminating in a tiny pinnacle at 65 m. A further 30 m of easier ground leads to the summit.
P. Mitchell, 31st May 1982.

Upper Couloir Keyhole   95 m   Grade III
To the right of the rib ascended by Capricorn, a snow bay cuts back into the upper rocks. Start at extreme left corner up steep snow aiming for an obvious chimney, short but hard when iced. Above 30 m of steep ground often iced, leads to a corner with a series of jammed boulders. Further steep ground narrows to a snow ridge that runs into easier ground above the finish of Capricorn. This route is technically more difficult than the Upper Couloir.
C. L. Donaldson and G. J. Dutton, March 1952.

North Face of North-east Spur   45 m   Grade III
This spur rises in a series of minor outcrops directly above the lochan. These outcrops give way to a steeper buttress and the climb goes up the centre of its north face with the angle easing at mid-height. There follows a pleasant snow arête that runs out on the summit ridge.
P. Mitchell, 31st May 1982.

Further north still where the rim of the ground between Sron nan Giubhas and Aonach Mór drops steeply into Coireach a' Bà, there are a number of short but steep gullies (concentrated in Coire Dhomhnaill of the 1:25,000 O.S. map: ref. NN232468). These were first climbed by J. H. B. Bell and Colin Allan and can be approached most conveniently from Bà Bridge.

Stob Dubh (883 m) and Beinn Ceitlein (832 m)

This twin-topped hill despite being dwarfed by its near neighbours on all sides, is easily recognised from lower Glen Etive by the gorge that cleaves the southern side of Stob Dubh and by the thumb (An Grianan) so prominent at the north-eastern extremity of Beinn Ceitlein above Alltchaorunn. It lies on the northern rim of the sea of Cruachan granite and is a complex of mica schist, quartzite, rhyolite and dykes of porphyry almost surrounded by granite.

The only straightforward approach is from Glenceitlein and either the west-south-west ridge of Stob Dubh can be ascended in a long, steep pull, or, the gorge itself can be scrambled up without difficulty. Ascent can also be made from Alltchaorunn leaving the track on the west side of the Allt a' Chaoruinn once well south of the thumb. This remarkable hump can be easily reached from the neck to its west, but otherwise should be avoided as its slopes are composed of rotten granite, heavily vegetated and at high angle. Its Gaelic name An Grianan is usually taken to mean a sunny place, a bower, but local opinion has it that the name relates to the similarity of the thumb to the shape in which peats or hay are stacked for drying.

Stob a' Choire Odhair (932 m), Beinn Toaig (827 m)

From near and far, through the western quadrant, Stob a' Choire Odhair with its satellite perched on an abutting shelf, shows a most distinctive shape. It blocks out Stob Ghabhar from the main road and is still prominent from the hills above Rannoch Station; while it appears as a graceful cone to those travelling the old road between the Black Mount summit and Bà Bridge. (The Gaelic pronunciation is something like Corryowa and from this has been derived the phoneticised English of Corrour).

A pleasant circuit can be made from Victoria Bridge using the track beside the Allt Toaig and the stalker's path that carries one gently on well-engineered zig-zags up most of the southern flank. This track starts a little over 2 km up the Allt Toaig at the point where a burn descends from an open gorge. Descent of Beinn Toaig's north-east ridge to the old road, gives a splendid view across Rannoch Moor being in line with the great fault occupied by Lochs Laidon and Ericht.

Clach Leathad (1098 m), Stob a' Ghlais Choire (996 m), Creise (1100 m), Meall a' Bhuiridh (1108 m)

Clach Leathad (pronounced Clachlyehat), the main peak in this group, makes a fine prospect when seen with its slightly higher satellite Meall a' Bhuiridh (pronounced Myowlavoori) from the A82. It looks even better from Bà Bridge and for a circuit of the two peaks, this is an ideal starting point. A little used track between the A82 and the old road provides the quickest approach: it starts a little beyond the main road bridge over the River Bà—here a link between Lochan na Stainge and Loch Bà—where parking space for cars is limited and much used by fishermen. This approach is equally convenient for an intended traverse from Meall a' Bhuiridh to Stob Ghabhar.

If Clach Leathad is the only peak to be climbed a pleasant circuit can be made and the splendour of Coireach a' Bà seen to advantage, by following the track on the north side of the River Bà until it runs out below a low-level promontory jutting out east from the southern flank of Clach Leathad. There is no avoiding the steepness of this flank which is prone to avalanche under fresh snow-fall, nor is there any easier-angled alternative available from the east. The east ridge is an obvious descent line but though well defined on the 1:50,000 O.S. map only experience of it on a clear day brings appreciation of its aerial nature, thrusting an elegant wedge out onto the moor.

All approaches from Glen Etive to the Black Mount group contrast remarkably in their enclosed nature to that sense of space given by Rannoch Moor; and, nowhere is this more epitomised than by the glen of the Allt Coire Ghuibhasan, which has the atmosphere of a Himalayan defile if not that scale. A good path clings to the steep slopes and is pleasantly shaded with birch and alder. From the Alltchaorunn bridge it keeps the east side of the burn and continues on the north side of the Allt Coire Guibhasan until crossing at a bridge. Further on there is a fine waterfall which has cut its way around a porphyry dyke and produced an abrupt right-angle turn behind a great sheaf of rock.

Once the glen opens out the most direct route to the summit climbs the steepening west ridge that flattens and curves north-wards over a wilderness of granite boulders. Alternatively, the bealach just east of Beinn Mhic Chasgaig can be reached and the broad spur climbed eastward to the top roughly $\frac{1}{2}$ km north of Clach Leathad. This top, known as Mam Coire Easain (1068 m)—which name applies more properly to the slopes north-east of and beneath it—is the point where the eastern escarpment is breached by relatively easy ground for descent to gain the west ridge of Meall a' Bhuiridh. Steep granite drops east along the length of the ridge between Clach Leathad and Creise but nowhere is the height great enough for worthwhile climbing. Beyond Mam Coire Easain the ridge continues north over Creise (1100 m)—pronounced Kraiesh—to a final eminence, Stob a' Ghlais Choire (996 m). This top together with its northern spur, Sron na Creise, presents a bold front to the north-east, seen to advantage from the lounge of the Kingshouse Hotel. In winter this view is breathtaking as its classical shape of buttresses containing apparently vertical gullies, holds a lot of snow. However, the viewpoint is misleading and all the open gullies can be climbed at Grade I standard, while the containing buttresses have also been climbed at moderate to difficult standard though the rock is not sound. Despite its forbidding appearance, Sron na Creise can also be climbed with no more than moderate scrambling on its north ridge. West of this ridge at an altitude of c. 600 m there is an exposure of steep, shattered rhyolite and were it not for the wealth of climbing across the glen, there might be more activity here.

Clach Leathad's western outlier Beinn Mhic Chasgaig (862 m) terminates above Alltchaorunn in a buttress of granite and two routes have been recorded here.

Surprise Pea   90 m   Very Severe
Start at foot of buttress and climb rib between two prominent
corners. Above overhang step left and continue diagonally left
to peg belay (36 m). Climb bulging slab above and continue
directly to large overlap, where go diagonally left past huge,
perched block and up to belay on sloping ledge (36 m). Finish up
rib above.
A. W. Ewing and A. McKeith, 29th October 1966.

Fish Finger   75 m   Very Severe
Ten metres up and right from lowest rocks, climb wall to grass
ledge and piton belay (9 m). Turn bulge onto sloping ledge and
climb prominent corner on nose of buttress to slabs and belay
below final wall (36 m). Finish over bulging slabs past a good
spike.
A. McKeith and A. W. Ewing, 29th October 1966.

The slab beneath and left of the buttress was also climbed by
A. McKeith.

Meall a' Bhuiridh (1108 m)

Easy slopes lead up from the old road near the ruin of Bà
Cottage. If descending the south-east ridge toward the minor
top, which has that same sense of isolation above the moor as
the other easterly ridges in the Black Mount, there is steep
craggy ground that needs a right-angled turn—either south-west
or north-west—to find easy ground. For those on their first visit
to the area and possibly seeking a quick route to the tops, Meall
a'Bhuiridh has a system of ski lift and tows starting a little above
the large car-park which is 1 km from the A82. The open corrie
above, Coire Pollach, has excellent snow-holding properties and
became the site in 1960 of Scotland's first commercial ski-ing
operation—The White Corries Ltd. The west-south-west ridge
forming a connection with the rest of the Clachlet group is
steeper and narrower than the 1:50,000 map indicates. In winter
it is prone to be icy, and a bad place to be without crampons.
A traverse of the Black Mount from Stob Ghabhar to Meall
a' Bhuiridh offers a splendid and full day for the hillwalker, with
the old road to leaven the afternoon dusk in winter. In reverse it
provides an equally fine day for the ski-mountaineer, who

would start the day from the top of Meall a' Bhuiridh by grace of the lift and tows above Blackrock Cottage and usually by returning as far as Bealach Fuar-chathaidh for descent into Coireach a' Ba. For a hillwalker this bealach is tricky to find in poor visibility, whichever direction it be approached from—for a skier descending the steep slope from Clach Leathad in such conditions and with the effort of maintaining equilibrium enough to occupy the mind, landing on the bealach will demand careful compass work.

This chapter closes fittingly with a reference to the Marchioness of Breadalbane whose book 'The High Tops of Blackmount' shows her deep appreciation of these hills and a refreshing respect for flora and fauna, despite her huge enjoyment of deer-stalking, for it was she who first recognised the need to preserve the Scots Pine about Loch Tulla and who had constructed the enclosure at Doire Darach (now under the supervision of the Nature Conservancy Council). She had also an immense respect for the stalkers and gillies employed in the Black Mount Forest, some of whom apparently had little time for the propriety of the day, as she engagingly recounts in stories at her own expense. One such concerns Sandy McLeish of Armaddy who when during one stalk was remonstrated with for speaking in Gaelic to the gillies, sharply rejoindered to his employer—'It is a pity you had not learned such a useful thing (Gaelic) before taking to the hill.'

Though out of print this book is well worth dredging from the Public Library system.

Accommodation

There are hotels at Bridge of Orchy and at Kingshouse. The former provides bunkhouse accommodation and is open all year round and the latter also offers bunkhouse accommodation but for group bookings only, while the hotel is closed for three months in the winter. The tradition of good hospitality is being maintained at the Inveroran where wooden spoons are no longer chained to the table as Neil Munro had it in the 'New Road'. This hotel usually closes in January and February and its limited accommodation makes advance booking a necessity. While there are no recognised camp-sites in the area, there is a long tradition of 'wild-camping' on the many flats in Glen Etive, as also on the flats beneath the Allt Tolaghan near Victoria Bridge. Recently an area of ground adjacent to Bridge of Orchy has been given over for camping and enquiries should be made at the Bridge of Orchy Hotel. Apart from the Glasgow University Mountaineering Club Hut 1.5 km west of Victoria Bridge, there is only one other hut and that is beautifully situated in Glen Etive and run by the Grampian Club at Inbhirfhaolain (pronounced Inver'oolan). To obtain details as to the current custodian, contact the Secretary of the Mountaineering Council of Scotland at 12, Douglas Crescent, Edinburgh. Blackrock Cottage is run by the Ladies Scottish Climbing Club.

References

The New Road, Neil Munro (O.P.).

The High Tops of Blackmount, the Marchioness of Breadalbane. Wm. Blackwood (1935) (O.P.).

Scottish Mountains on Ski, Malcolm Slesser, West Col. (1970).

Always a Little Further, Alastair Borthwick. John Smith (1983). Contains a fine account of climbing the Upper Couloir in pre-war times.

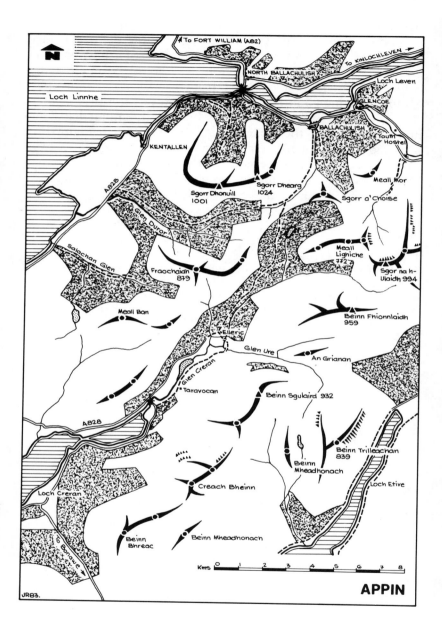

27. *Beinn Sgulaird from the east.*   *Peter Hodgkiss*

28. *Beinn Fhionnlaidh and Sgór na h'Ulaidh's two tops from upper Glen Ceitlein.*
                                                        Peter Hodgkiss

29.　The deeply shadowed cone of Beinn Trilleachan from the pastures of Armaddy—once known as the granary of Loch Etive.

Peter Hodgkiss

30.   *From Bidean nam Bian: Fraochaidh is right of centre, and left of centre, the faint shape of Ben More on Mull can be made out. Hard left, the shaded north face of Sgor na h'Ulaidh lies behind the sunlit ridge of Aonach Dubh a' Ghlinne.*   *Peter Hodgkiss*

31. Beinn Sgulaird from the birch-wood fringe above Glen Creran.   *Peter Hodgkiss*

32.   Beinn a' Bheithir from Stob Coire nan Lochan.

32a.   Beinn a' Bheithir from the south face of Bidean nam Bian.   Peter Hodgkiss

33. *Sgór na h'Ulaidh from the slopes above Glen Creran. Taken 20 years ago before the trees grew.* *Peter Hodgkiss*

34. *Buachaille Etive Mór from Blackrock Cottage. The line of the Chasm can be seen above the right-hand gable-end.* *Peter Hodgkiss*

35.   Pitch 4: The Chasm.   P. S. Orr

36. *Stob Dearg of Buachaille Etive Mór.*   *Peter Hodgkiss*

5

Appin

Beinn Mheadhonach (714 m)
Beinn Malurgainn (692 m)
Beinn Bhreac (708 m)
Creach Bheinn (810 m)
*__Beinn Sgulaird__ (932 m)
Beinn Trilleachan (839 m)
*__Beinn Fhionnlaidh__ (959 m)
*__Sgor na h'Ulaidh__ (994 m)
Fraochaidh (879 m)
Beinn a' Bheithir
*__Sgorr Dhearg__ (1024 m)
*__Sgòrr Dhonuill__ (1001 m)
Sgòrr Bhàn (901 m)

Unlike neighbouring areas to the east and north-east, Appin and Barcaldine contain few large, mountainous hills: correspondingly fewer people will be met, particularly on the lower hills in the southern half of the district. Its major glens are heavily afforested with much recent planting, but have also a spread of healthy oak in Glen Creran and a fine birch wood on the eastern slopes of Beinn Trilleachan. To the west good tracks intersect Appin, both commencing at Ballachulish, the one veering west through Glen Duror and the other leading south over a low pass to Loch Creran; but the expanse of Barcaldine bordered by Loch Creran, Gleann Salach and Loch Etive contains but a few, minor hill-paths.

There is major rock-climbing on the great plaque of rough, granite slabs on Beinn Trilleachan's east face and, on a lesser scale, some caving in the bands of limestone that run through Glen Creran. Near the southern tip of Barcaldine the quarry at Bonawe is a curiosity, its face seamed with rich colours of pink and purple, while adjacent to it sits incongruously a single tenement, presumably built for the quarry workers who hewed

67

sets for Glasgow's pavements. An early and far-sighted visitor, Thomas Pennant, reported in 1769 his fear that the iron-foundry at Bunaw (sic) would soon devour the beautiful woods of the country.

Beinn Mheadhonach (714 m), Beinn Malurgainn (692 m), Beinn Bhreac (708 m)

For those who do not count altitude too highly in their choice of hills, this round of rough and unfrequented country involves five tops and a longer day than the 15 km distance might suggest. It gives fine views of the sea lochs Creran and Etive and of Lismore stretched across both their exits. Gleann Salach, which is a continuation of the curving fault-line so apparent in the Pass of Brander, provides a central starting point at its summit and a little north of the River Esragan. This river is powerful in spate and even without that condition, is not easily crossed dry-shod near the road. Beinn Bhreac carries an unusually large summit cairn but nothing else is so prominent in this round and the three bealachs between Beinn Malurgainn and Beinn Mheadhonach (the middle hill; pronounced Veea'nach) are not easily found in thick weather.

Creach Bheinn (810 m)

This twin-topped hill can be included in the round from Beinn Bhreac to Beinn Mheadhonach or climbed singly from Dallachulish near the disused railway bridge. The recent afforestation stretches no more than $\frac{1}{2}$ km up the west ridge and it is worth hunting for the firebreaks, best found on the north where deciduous woodland clothes the lower slopes, so that the ridge can be followed. In descent pleasant variety will be found on a line west-north-west from the southern top—in order to cross the gorge of Eas Garbh with its fine waterfall.

Beinn Lora (305 m)

This small eminence in Benderloch lies in the westernmost corner of the Central Highlands and it can be climbed comfortably in an hour from North Ledaig, which is rather oddly south of Ledaig itself. The whole northern aspect of the hill is afforested and though a track runs through the forest, the southern approach gives more open views. There is an outlook of some splendour from this minor hill which has an unrestricted view across to the Sound of Mull and down the Firth of Lorn. An evening visit is particularly worthwhile for the sunset behind Mull.

Beinn Sgulaird (932 m)

Standing as it does, at the head of a sea loch, Beinn Sgulaird gives a fine western panorama of scattered islands backed by almost the whole extent of Mull. To the east there is stark contrast in Beinn Trilleachan's scaly eastern aspect and an intervening moor of peat hags.

The approach first described is not the most direct but does allow a circuit including a traverse of Beinn Trilleachan's north-south summit ridge. It uses an ancient path running over from the head of Loch Etive to Glenure in Glen Creran, that is not marked on the O.S. 1:50,000 map. However, a start from the southern extremity of the afforestation allows one to pick up the traces. With shallow soil cover on the underlying granite this path can be very wet and a crossing in such conditions lends respect for the missionary preachers of the last century who used it all year round in order to read the service each second Sunday to the isolated parish in Glen Etive. Beinn Sgulaird's eastern ridge over the intervening Stob Gaibhre (684 m) ascends unmistakably out of the moor and higher, as it begins to trend south, can be made an enjoyable scramble on sound granite.

From Glen Creran the most direct route starts at the road-end where there is car parking space at the farm of Elleric. A land rover track to Glenure House, crosses the River Ure and continues up the south side to a bifurcation west of Stob Gaibhre. Above to the south a long steep pull leads to the neck west of Stob Gaibhre. There is fine scenery in the wooded gorge cut by the River Ure through beds of granite, limestone, and schist, and the path to the twin lochans, Airigh nan Lochan, makes a pleasanter approach than that up the steep slope to the south.

A second route from the west starts at Druimavuic and

follows the west ridge thrown down from Beinn Sgulaird's southern top (856 m).

Many small outcrops of granite appear on the northern slopes of Stob Gaibhre and of Beinn Sgulaird's north top, but the only recorded climbing occurs on the two areas of pink, granite slabs which are exposed on the western slope of Beinn Sgulaird's south-south-west ridge at NN 051455 and below the shallow bealach at the foot of the ridge.

The main slabs are about 180 m high and are composed of solid, clean granite. In the centre are large overlaps with good cracks for nuts. Above the main slab is the Upper Slab, while over on the right is the Bealach Crag, and on its right, below, the Lower Bealach Slabs. The best and longest climbs are on the Main Slab and are described from left to right. Peg belays are required on most routes which were all first climbed by G. N. Hunter and N. Quinn in September 1976.

Safari   195 m   Hard Severe
Start at arrow on lowest rock on left of slab. Climb slab direct then trend left to belay (45 m). Follow large slab corner, move left to belay on small ledge (40 m). Climb left then right above large semi-detached blocks to belay on right (27 m). Continue directly up smooth slab above, move left then up through overlaps, follow slab above to second overlap, break through and follow good cracks to belay (45 m). Move up leftwards into corner then up through overlap to finish up crest of ridge (36 m).

Majuba   160 m   Severe
Start at arrow on lowest rocks. Climb slab direct (45 m). Continue directly up slab right of corner then trend right to small overlap, which break through on right, climb left then directly to belay (42 m). Climb corner above direct to large overlaps, break through crack and grooves to belay on small stance (27 m). Continue directly via grooves and small overlap to terminal overlap and climb this directly to finish (45 m).

Tokalosh   167 m   Very Severe
Start right of Majuba. Climb easy rounded slab to belay (45 m). Trend right to bow-shaped corner on central slab, climb to top of corner, step right onto thin slab, up then trend left to shallow scoop and up to belay (45 m). Climb steep grooves above thin

slab to belay below large overlaps (30 m). Climb up corner, large blocks, climb overhang into grooves, follow these directly to rock nose then small corner slab. Belay under blocks at grass ledge (45 m).

Assegai   158 m   Very Severe
Start at arrow on right of slab. Climb easy corner on slab to grass patch, climb overlap above to belay (45 m). Climb grooves above (42 m). Continue up steep slab and grooves (42 m). Finish up corner groove above (27 m).

Upper Slabs

The following two routes climb the two obvious curving faults through overlaps in a series of steps.

39 Steps   91 m   Severe
This is the left fault. Start at arrow, follow small corners trending left to belay (51 m). Follow cracks and grooves right, climb up and through overlaps (40 m).

Tiptoe   91 m   Severe
Start at arrow. Climb obvious fault line right of 39 Steps in the centre of the slab. Break through overlaps on good holds.

Bealach Crag

Creran Corner   72 m   Severe
Climb directly up into obvious large corner, follow this to belay on ledge (40 m). Climb slab to overlap, trend right to second overlap then slab above to belay on ledge (24 m). Climb wall above belay to finish.

Beinn Trilleachan (839 m)

Few Scottish hills outside Skye show such extensive exposure of rock as this hill's western aspect. Oddly the eastern slopes above Loch Etive where occur the deservedly renowned 'Etive Slabs', are steeper but more vegetated. Indeed the angle of the eastern slope is not appreciated until viewed from north or south, when also the ridge-like shape of the hill becomes apparent. The top is easily reached from the head of Loch Etive, starting up the path described under Beinn Sgulaird, but rather than ascending and returning by the north-north-east ridge, a circuit of it and the north-north-west ridge is more repaying. On the west face of this latter ridge and a little north of Lochan an Lair, there is a sweep of granite steeper and of greater vertical length than the mass of rock exposed hereabout. Those who tire of the weekend crowds on the 'Etive Slabs' might find worthwhile climbing here.

The ridge between Beinn Trilleachan and its northern top, Meall nan Gobhar, makes a splendid walk over tors and warts of granite, with a spectacular drop to Loch Etive on one side and the angle here too steep for any sight of the 'Etive Slabs'. Those wishing to climb on these slabs will find the best routes described in K. V. Crockett's *Glencoe and Glen Etive*.

Less serious entertainment can be found roughly 3 km south of the 'Etive Slabs', in the 'The Chasm' of Beinn Trilleachan. This is the right-hand fork of a gully divided by an obvious dark tongue of rock (Teanga Dubh—pronounced Tyeng'a Doo). There are no unavoidable difficulties but good sport can be had and the rock scenery is spectacular. The first recorded ascent was by I. Rowe and G. Tiso in 1973.

Beinn Fhionnlaidh (959 m)

Confusion is often expressed as to the pronunciation of this name relative to that of its neighbour Sgor na h'Ulaidh and, so near as the author is able to phoneticise Gaelic speech, the difference is something like the following: Beinn Fhionnlaidh pronounced HiönlY with the initial 'h' not well heard and Sgor na h'Ulaidh pronounced HoolY (some local people have been known to confuse the issue even further by pronouncing the initial 'f' of Fhionnlaidh out of consideration for incomers).

About the peak's fine stature there is no doubt, though it is hidden from most viewpoints and appears to have been largely ignored by early mountaineers, there being only three references to it in Vols I–XXVII of the SMC Journal.

From Glen Creran a path, not marked on the O.S. 1:50,000 First Series map, leads from north of Glenure House across the southern flank of the hill. For the most straightforward ascent, the path should be left after 2 km and a line east-north-east taken to gain a prominent shoulder on the west ridge. A more interesting route can be made by following the path to Lochan na h'Uraich, 1 km beyond which a gully with a fine waterfall splits the southern flank. To the right of the gully a series of crags offer scrambling for 200 m and lead to the final slopes south of the cairn.

There is a similar distance from Glen Etive but no route through the extensive afforestation is shown on the O.S. 1:50,000 First Series map. Starting at Invercharnan House a Forestry Commission track winds south and then west through the forest for 3 km until a fire-break is found when the track doubles back east. This is the only straightforward route through the forest. Beyond a stretch of wet moor leads to steep slopes beneath an eastern satellite (841 m). These slopes are easily avoided by keeping due west to the neck north of another minor top (595 m).

To the north Beinn Fhionnlaidh presents a truly mountainous appearance and in winter the open corrie beneath the summit offers general mountaineering and particularly so about the steep crag high on the eastern flank of the corrie. Further east the satellite top (841 m) throws down a ridge north-north-east that is interrupted by a number of steps. These are not easy to descend in winter with the easier, turning movements to the right also on steep ground.

At the tail of Beinn Fhionnlaidh's south-eastern flank above Glen Etive, a small top known as Creag Dubh (301 m) has some worthwhile climbing at Severe and harder on a steep, granite crag of perhaps 30 m height. The crag is well seen from the road near Drumachoish and facing south-east it dries out quickly.

Sgor na h'Ulaidh (994 m)

As with Beinn Fhionnlaidh, this hill is also hidden from distant view while even from adjacent tops, its complex of ridges makes appreciation of its shape difficult. In winter only one of the routes described below should not present difficulty—that by Meall a'Bhuiridh from Glen Etive—while, particularly in descent, all others will require care.

The hill's finest feature—Coire Dubh with its two steep gullies—is revealed only to those who approach by Gleann Leac na Muidhe. This glen commences from the A82 2 km west of

Loch Achtriochtan, where a private road follows the west side of the burn for 1½ km to the farm of Gleann-leac-na-muidhè itself. From the lower reaches of this track, on a clear winter's day, there is a splendid view of Aonach Eagach, its wall-like front to Glencoe and its turreted crest showing to great effect.

Beyond the farm a path continues on the east side of the burn for a little way and just beyond the point where a large tributary joins the Allt na Muidhe from the west, there is a footbridge. The upper reaches of the glen are confined and much riven by drainage and little is gained by contouring either slope until almost beneath the north face, from where a bealach to the west is quickly gained and steep slopes climbed south to the western shoulder, Corr na Beinne.

An alternative route from Gleann Leac na Muidhe starts directly from the farm up the steep slopes of Aonach Dubh a'Ghlinne (the dark ridge of the glen, and well-named, showing a dark front to the north with profound glens on either side) which gives a superb aerial highway to a fore-top, **Stob an Fhuarain** (968 m). From this ridge the view is largely curtailed by the mass of Bidean nan Bian but the majesty of the latter's south face, particularly when covered in snow, is consolation enough. Beyond a drop of 200 m leads to a neck beneath the final, steep ridge.

The extensive afforestation on the western slopes of Glen Etive leaves only one gap for access to Sgor na h'Ulaidh, and this 1½ km south of the sharp bend at Inbhir-fhaolain, where the edge of the forest can be followed into Glenn Charnan and thus to the Bealach Fhionnghaill. Above steep slopes, interrupted by short but vertical steps, lead again to the fore-peak of Stob an Fhuarain. In icy conditions descent of this slope demands great care for turning movements to the right are not easily found and are themselves on steep ground. A second approach from Glen Etive can be made by using the Forestry Commission track behind Invercharnan House, taking the first right turn perhaps 190 m beyond the house. When the track runs out, the quickest way through the forest is due west onto the slopes of Meall a'Bhuiridh (748 m). Pleasant walking follows over schist pavements and higher over knolls until easy slopes lead down to a rocky bealach and Sgor na h'Ulaidh's south-east ridge. No difficulty need be encountered on this ridge which is a much easier option for winter descent than that to the Bealach Fhionnghaill.

Glen Creran can also be used for approach but the track beyond Elleric, shown on the O.S. 1:50,000 First Series map, Sheet 50, leading to Salachail runs out leaving a 2 km struggle through the afforestation. Better is the track from Glenure House that runs above and east of the River Creran and this track is marked on the O.S. 1:50,000 Second Series map, Sheet 41, but not on Sheet 50. This path also runs out and leaves a stony hillside to be traversed to a crossing of the river beneath the steep ground falling from Corr na Beinne. In dry summer weather an alternative here is to cross the River Creran 2 km beyond the end of the track to a clearing in the forest, from where the bed of the Allt Easain provides a pleasant way through the trees and on to the bealach between Sgor na h'Ulaidh and Meall Lighiche.

Coire Dubh contains three winter climbs one of which, Red Gully, is of high quality: all are hidden from view until one is in the higher reaches of Gleann Leac na Muidhe and then ascent to the east is needed before the left-hand aspect of the face can be studied.

Vixen Gully   260 m   Grade I
This is the prominent snow-gully with a distinctive hour-glass shape. Early and late in winter the narrows at half-height can have a short rock step.

Red Gully   220 m   Grade III
A little to the left of Vixen Gully and directly beneath the summit a shallow gully cuts through broken crags. Always difficult but more variable than many gullies at this grade, there is usually a rope-length at mid-height on iced rock.

Start up snow-fan steepening to a 10 m ice-pitch. Above very steep snow, often broken with rock steps, leads to a corner on the left. Climb the corner for 30 m. Now move right into a recess and climb a steep wall, 15 m. Finish up steep snow leading almost to the cairn.
D. Scott, J. C. Henderson and R. Anderson, February 1950.

Subsidiary Scoop   160 m   Grade II
Immediately left of Red Gully and separated from it by a rock

rib is a steep scoop of snow interrupted by short ice steps.
Mr. and Mrs. I. Clough, March 1966.

On the right-hand aspect of the face almost directly above the
bealach between Creag Bhàn and Sgor na h'Ulaidh, a snow gully
sweeps up among fine rock scenery steepening at the top.
J. G. Parish, D. H. Haworth and J. S. Berkely, February 1948.

Creag Bhàn (719 m)

This northern wing of Meall Lighiche (772 m) provides another
winter climb above Gleann Leac na Muidhe with an obvious
gully of 300 m to the right of the top.

Humpback Gully   300 m   Grade II
J. Renny, I. MacEacheran, R. Sharp and W. Sproul, November
1965.

Fraochaidh (879 m)

The Gaelic meaning of this name, which in Appin is pronounced
Free'achy, means heathery hill, but its aptness can no longer be
appreciated until high up as the hill is now almost surrounded
by afforestation. There are however views to be had out of
proportion to Fraochaidh's relatively minor stature for it provides unrestricted sighting down Loch Linnhe and in winter
from the lochan east of the minor top Meall Bàn, Beinn
a'Bheithir takes on an Alpine scale.

Approach from Ballachulish involves a long walk up Gleann
an Fhiodh but gives fine views down Glen Creran and pleasant
going over knolly ground on the north-eastern wing. The left-
fork roughly 3½ km from Ballachulish that leads south-south-
west to the pass over to Glen Creran, is faint and easily missed.

The shortest route starts from Duror using the Forestry
Commission track that runs east from a little north of the Duror
Inn. After 3 km follow a fire-break down to the River Duror and
hunt for a gated bridge (NM 023536). Above the afforestation
gives out at mid-height and a broad ridge leads to the top.

Salachan Glen is now too heavily afforested for approach over
Meall Bàn, but is mentioned for the discovery of caves there. A
band of limestone runs from the south-west up Glen Stockdale

and through to Glen Duror and an entrance to a cave-system has been found above the farm-house at Bealach where, on the edge of the recent afforestation, a large burn disappears underground beside an old tree.

Beinn a'Bheithir

Sgorr Dhearg (1024 m), Sgòrr Dhonuill (1001 m)

Dropping as it does, so steeply into Loch Leven, the bulk and grandeur of this hill—pronounced Vair—is not properly appreciated until one is on the north side of the loch. However, the sight from Ballachulish of Sgorr Dhearg's outlier Sgòrr Bhàn under a coat of snow that highlights the horizontal strata prominent under the summit cone, gives a sense of scale and steepness not too much exaggerated.

The three main tops together with a remote and lower top to the north-west (Creag Ghorm, 758 m), form a north-facing horse-shoe with an apparently isolated tower jutting out from east of Sgòrr Dhonuill. The whole of the glen contained by this horseshoe holds afforestation of a maturity, and forestry tracks in number, to confound any stranger descending unawares. Those who plan a circuit of these tops using Gleann a'Chaolais for descent, should work out their route carefully and reach the treeline in daylight. Two crucial sections of the forestry tracks are described.

For approach to both a car can be driven ½ km up the glen using the metalled road signposted to Glenachulish. To reach the foot of Sgorr Dhearg's north ridge, which narrows as it gains height but maintains an easy angle, cross the main burn by a bridge and climb open slopes east-south-east to a corner in the forest edge, where a track will be found running through the forest. Follow this north-east and then east to the first burn where the forest is shallow enough for a quick passage. In descent the same burn is the best landmark.

Starting the circuit from Creag Ghorm the track on the west side of the main burn should be followed for 1 km until a small dam can be seen to the left, when the first right turn should be taken. At the third angle of the zig-zags and nearing the second crossing of a burn, strike up through the trees due west. Above open slopes are soon reached. Very recent felling in this area can only have made this approach easier.

A pleasanter way of making the traverse, though it may involve use of the Oban to Inverness bus service, is to ascend Sgòrr Bhàn from Ballachulish, either due west to gain its north-north-east ridge or by following the path south until the east-north-east ridge towers overhead. This latter ridge is a splendid mountain route, ever-steepening until rock steps on clean quartzite require use of the hands: in winter these rock steps ice up readily and can be trying.

Beyond Sgòrr Bhàn the ridge to Sgorr Dhearg forms a most graceful arc under snow and further on the east ridge of Sgorr Dhonuill narrows and often forms an arête in winter. Under such conditions it is well worth diverging half-way up Sgorr Dhonuill to follow the even narrower arête leading north to Sgòrr a'Chaolais—the tower or horn so conspicuous from the main road. Its isolated position some distance out into the corrie gives it a splendid arc of view.

For distant views of loch and hill, Beinn a'Bheithir's summit outlook is hard to match; there being a telescoping effect as one looks into the narrows of Loch Leven and Glencoe that adds to the stature of the hills, while to the south-west the length of Loch Linnhe opens out to the sea beyond Mull.

From Creag Ghorm a descent can be made steeply but forest-free, to Kentallen whose tranquil bay was observed by Dorothy Wordsworth to be sheltered from 'half the winds that travel over the lake' and where accordingly Neil Munro had Para Handy put in for shelter and refreshment. Close to the road the course of the dismantled railway line now carries enormous bramble bushes with appropriately giant berries.

The vast southern flank of Beinn a'Bheithir will attract few; the afforestation making an unpleasant barrier and the slopes above being tiresomely steep. However for those staying at Duror of Appin and determined to investigate this aspect of the hill, there is consolation in the entertaining scramble to be had in the gully leading up to the west of Sgòrr Dhonuill's final slope. It starts at c. 550 m and narrows higher where the granite rockwalls are impressive. The approach through the forest described under Fraochaidh should be followed and the same fire-break taken, this time uphill, to a clearing at the top corner of which another fire-break leads through to open slopes. At the forest edge a line due north, traversing a little left and crossing two burns, puts one in the line of the gully. On the O.S. 1:50,000 Sheet 41, it is the last gully shown to the west under Sgorr Dhonuill's west ridge.

Cross-country routes

Two routes of century-long usage run roughly south to north; the one on the eastern fringe beside Loch Etive and the other cutting through from Glen Creran to Ballachulish. Both make fine low-level walks.

Loch Etive

The eastern shore of Loch Etive has the greater distance and in wet weather the shallow soil on the skirts of Beinn Trilleachan becomes saturated. However there is a good track as far as Barrs and there is a grand wildness to the scenery across the loch: then there is the attractive prospect of using the steamer for return (by prior arrangement—see Introduction, page 2).

Remnants of oak linger south of Cadderlie near where was the school at one time, showing how the population has been reduced more than the oak woods. Roughly 1 km south of Cadderlie springs bubble up haphazardly at the side of the loch, as they do on the opposite shore at Inverliver. Near Barrs charcoal beds can be found east of the Allt Easach and, further on through the policies of the house, the old pier sits out over very deep water that is salt to the taste. South and north of Barrs and, beside the burns on Beinn Trilleachan's lower slopes, regiments of conifers have been planted, merging uneasily with the parkland about Barrs and with the hazel groves on Beinn Trilleachan.

The richness of bird life makes May and June rewarding months for this walk and if one leaves the path to tread the shingle, there is some risk of stepping on a sand-piper's nest, so numerous are these delightful waders. Beyond Barrs the view across the loch into the glens draining Ben Starav, has a quality of wildness usually associated with mountainous land on a larger scale.

Glen Creran

A right of way maintained through the new forests of conifers, connects this glen with Ballachulish and provides easy access to a small, but shapely hill, Sgorr a'Choise (663 m). From the road end at Elleric a great stretch of trees has been planted by the Forestry Commission and these reach up to the pass crossed by the path, curtailing much of the view.

The lower reaches of the glen are rich in human history with one instance—the shooting of one of HM Tax Collectors some 200 years ago—perpetuated by Robert Louis Stevenson in his book *Kidnapped*. This incident has its place in Scottish history for the acknowledged wrongful hanging of James Stewart of Duror after conviction for the shooting by a court working out clan bias rather than process of law. Recent researchers have suggested that, contrary to accepted belief, the tax collector—one Colin Campbell known as the Red Fox—was not shot by Jacobites out of resentment at his Government duties, but was killed by a hired assassin. This theory has it that Colin Campbell was at odds with fellow conspirators, who were highly placed in Scottish affairs of the time, over the share-out of misappropriated French gold (originally shipped to Scotland to finance the Jacobite Cause).

In recent times extensive cave-systems have been discovered in the band of limestone that courses up the glen from the lochside almost to the summit of Fraochaidh, though the Gaelic name Uamh Coire Sheilach—uamh being the Gaelic for a cave—given to the site suggests that A. MacKeith's first recorded descents in 1973 may have been predated by a century or two. The entrances will be found above and inside the oak wood of Coille Mheadhonach at NN 034494 and NN 030496, but the extent of the limestone and other, parallel bands nearby suggests the likelihood of further discoveries. In detail the burn falling behind the schoolhouse should be followed to a fork and the left fork taken to its second waterfall: 12 m up and then 15 m left should find the entrance in amongst birch trees. There is an initial descent by abseil of 45 m and a total passage known to date of c. 300 m. The second entrance will be found 400 m further up the burn and 15 m left at the edge of the wood.

Those wishing to potter among the old woods in the lower

reaches of the glen may find interest in the disused limekiln beside the road at NN 004456—where local limestone was crushed and burned to produce fertiliser—and in the old lead-mines above Invercreran.

Accommodation

See previous chapter, page 64. There are hotels at South Ballachulish and at Duror of Appin, and bed and breakfast accommodation in the same area. Local tourist office—telephone 08552 296.

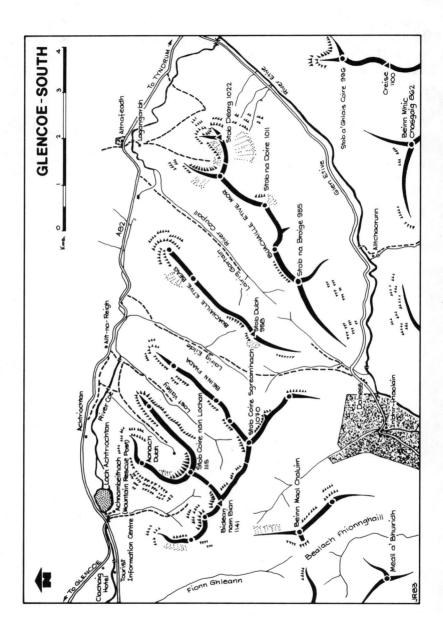

GLENCOE - SOUTH

37.   *From Am Bodach of Aonach Eagach: looking west down Glencoe to Beinn a' Bheithir (right).*

Peter Hodgkiss

38.   *Stob Coire nan Lochan. Broad Gully is the longest stretch of snow running up to the right of the peak.*

W. A. Bentall

39. From Aonach Eagach: the Bidean range above the steep northern flanks of Aonach Dubh. *Peter Hodgkiss*

40. Newly born deer calf; Coire Gabhail. *Peter Hodgkiss*

41.   *Stob Coire nan Lochan's white cone towers aloof behind the 'Three Sisters'.*

Peter Hodgkiss

42.   *Bidean nam Bian with its Diamond and Church-door Buttresses.*   *Alastair MacGregor*

43. The length of Aonach Eagach from Meall Mór. Clachaig Gully slants up to the left skirted by the obvious scar of the badly eroded path. Peter Hodgkiss

44. *Am Bodach of Aonach Eagach from the mouth of Coire nan Lochan.* *Peter Hodgkiss*

6

Glencoe

*Buachaille Etive Mór—Stob Dearg (1022 m)
   Stob na Doire (1011 m)
   Stob Coire Altruim (939 m)
   Stob na Broige (955 m)
*Buachaille Etive Beag—Stob Dubh (958 m)
   Stob Coire Raineach (925 m)
*Bidean nam Bian (1150 m)
   Stob Coire nam Beith (1107 m)
   Stob Coire nan Lochan (1115 m)
   Stob Coire Sgreamhach (1072 m)
   Beinn Fhada (952 m)

The magnificent scenery of this glen is such that its name is renowned internationally and has achieved that indiscriminate use in advertising accorded only to the world's wonders: discerning early travellers, such as the Wordsworths, and Victorian artists, such as Thomas Miles Richardson, were enraptured by its dramatic appearance and today few people will not have seen some calendar picture of it. Despite this cultural exposure, few first-time visitors will be quite prepared for the shock of the first view, whether from west or east, whether in fair weather or foul, when from the south the three huge buttresses seem almost to be pushing across the narrow bed of the glen to rest against the vast flank of the Aonach Eagach.

From a vantage point above the road at the Meeting of the Three Waters it is easy to imagine the cataclysmic forces underlying the dramatic forms before one. For the hills fronting onto the glen are part of an island of igneous rock—the remains of successive lava flows that spilled out more than 300 million years ago. Most of these have been eroded down to the underlying metamorphic rock but an area 14 × 8 km collapsed within a ring fracture and was subsequently protected from erosion so

D

that it now stands proud. Next glaciation ground out soft rock in the bed of the glen leaving Bidean's three ridges, composed of more resistant rocks, with the truncated spurs that now seem to impend over the glen. One of the these more resistant rocks is the rhyolite that gives such sound and impeccable material for rock-climbing on Buachaille Etive Mór's Stob Dearg and on the west face of Aonach Dubh. Today the glen is tamed by a main road but stormy weather can still unleash forces that belittle man's efforts and after Christmas 1980 heavy rain and an overnight thaw of deep snow brought down boulders from the Aonach Eagach that blocked the road not far from the place where the village of Achtriochtan was inundated and then abandoned in the 18th century.

Since 1937 the glen and much of the high ground about it, has been owned by the National Trust—not surprisingly this area agrees closely with the boundary of the ancient ring-fracture. Prior to 1937 piece-meal purchases had brought such prizes as Bidean nam Bian under the National Trust's wing, but in that year Dalness Forest, including Buachaille Etive Mòr and Buachaille Etive Beag, came on the market and sufficient money was raised on an initiative by the SMC to provide the National Trust with the purchase price. Percy Unna was the driving force behind this magnificent gift to all hill-goers of the future: he had the foresight to seize the opportunity, the conviction needed to persuade others to contribute—substantial contributions from 20 English clubs and 319 other contributions from south of the border; a large sum from the Pilgrim Trust; and £1160 from his fellow SMC members—and the generosity to make the largest individual contribution from his own purse. His fund-raising circular contained a passage worth quoting in this guide—it stated that 'it was intended that the Trust (the National Trust) should be asked to undertake that the land should be maintained in its primitive condition for all time'.

In the Central Highlands there are larger peaks more remote from main roads, but no other range is so generally mountainous, nor demands so readily in winter, mountaineering techniques for the simplest ascents. Using the expressive terminology of Dr. Marion Newbigin, who in a most readable article about land-form (SMC *Journal*, Vol. XIII, p. 124) maligned Scottish hills in a general comparison with other mountain ranges, as 'suet dumplings scantily provided with plums', the major peaks about Glencoe are bare, Damson stones!

From November until April and, even later in hard winters, its ridges sharpen into arêtes and carry large cornices and though the proximity of the Atlantic brings mid-winter thaws that can strip snow even from the highest points, these sudden changes in temperatures also turn easy ground into icy slopes that seem somehow to have increased in angle. Some experience in the use of crampons and an ice-axe on steep ground, and the ability to navigate in adverse conditions are advised for those planning their first winter visit.

Buachaille Etive Mór—Stob Dearg (1022 m)

One of the finest views in the Central Highlands can be had from a main road. It lies in wait for those driving north on the A82 where, after its crest, the road veers west and ahead, out of the flat expanse of Rannoch Moor, Stob Dearg springs up uncompromisingly, steep enough to show bare rock in most winter conditions and of a warm, pink hue in summer light. Well did Principal Shairp describe its front to the moor as a 'furrowed visage' for it is seamed with gullies and buttressed by a complex of pillars not easily separated by the eye unless there is early-morning light.

No Scottish peak is more redolent of early rock-climbing history than Stob Dearg—Norman Collie, with Solly and Collier, made his eponymous climb up the east face in 1895, a route described by J. H. B. Bell as 'an old and superior vintage which is best tasted AND SAVOURED in very dry winter conditions'; Harold Raeburn left his mark, with the first ascent, in winter at that, of Crowberry Gully; and the ubiquitous Abrahams came north to pick up the plum of Crowberry Ridge. Almost all the rock on Stob Dearg's front to the moor is rhyolite, sound and clean and with small incut holds on its steeper parts. K. V. Crocket's selective guide *Glencoe and Glen Etive* includes the best routes for those wishing to rock-climb here, but this guide would be incomplete without some detail of two easy mountaineering routes and one mountaineering expedition.

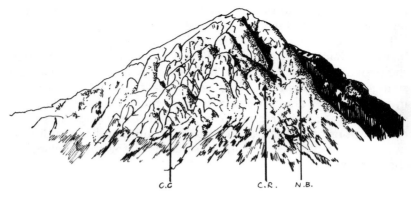

Stob Dearg of Buachaille Etive Mór

C.C. Collie's Climb
C.R. Curved Ridge
N.B. North Buttress

Curved Ridge is a moderate rock-climb that makes a logical and direct route to the summit: it winds through splendid rock scenery and offers dress-circle seats for the rock-climbs on the Rannoch Wall. The foot of the rocks can be approached either across the flank of Stob Dearg from Lagangarbh or more directly across the river Coupal via the stepping stones under the car-park 1 km west of the Glen Etive road-end: both approaches converge below a conspicuous water-streaked slab, and neither avoids the steep upper path of scree. Despite the great scar of this path, the foot of the ridge is not easily found, since countless feet have diverged looking for firmer footing and to avoid steep ground. Two features help in arriving at the start of the climb. Roughly 160 m above the water-streaked slab a steepening and lofty wall on the left pushes the path rightward until it traverses horizontally into a recess with an often. greasy step up to the right leading to open ground again. Above a bay receiving drainage from gullies on either side of Crowberry Ridge, should be skirted to the left, leading soon to the route. After 250 m of alternate walking and steep scrambling on sound rock, the ridge flattens to merge into the hillside beneath the Crowberry Tower and scree should be followed rightward to a neck behind the Tower—in a fine situation at the top of *Crowberry Gully*—from where a short, steep scramble leads to the summit slopes.

Another fine mountaineering route is the *North Buttress* and it is reached by a rising traverse rightward from the foot of the bay beneath Crowberry Ridge. When steep rock is reached easier ground directly above leads to a broad terrace that girdles the Buttress. The best climbing will be found up an obvious system of cracks and open chimneys at the centre of the arc made by the girdle: it is nowhere harder than Difficult. Those visiting Stob Dearg for the first time would be amply repaid by following the terrace to the west side of the buttress where there is a breath-taking view down into Great Gully and up into Raven's Gully.

Last is recommended the *Chasm*, which ranks as one of the finest mountaineering expeditions in the British Isles. Its rock scenery is superb, the route finding is complex, and the difficulty of the climbing together with the majesty of the surroundings increases with height until the final awesome pitch above the Devil's Cauldron. Most recently this expedition has been realistically graded Very Severe in K. V. Crocket's *Selective Guide*, for even after a drought the harder pitches near the top are wet. It will be found roughly $1\frac{1}{2}$ km down the Glen Etive Road, where a flat, wooden road-bridge is a good landmark for those in a car, and is the most obvious gully on this south-eastern aspect of Stob Dearg: climbing commences at c. 400 m. Many of the early Scottish climbers were drawn to it returning after repeated defeats and writing in awe of its obstacles—Harold Raeburn with Willie Ling in April 1906 made an ascent, using the 'South Wall' exit, which was disallowed since many of the pitches were buried under snow (these had previously been led by Raeburn in 1903)—and it took 22 years before the first complete ascent was made by R. F. Stobart and Mr. and Mrs. N. E. Odell in April 1920. A winter ascent is a prize worth patient observation and is more often achievable than is generally realised; though both in difficulty and in form, the individual pitches are extraordinarily variable. In March 1979 (18.3.79) the '100 ft Wall' pitch—a wall of more than 100 ft at an angle of c. 75°—was completely banked out and had become a steep but straightforward slope of hard snow, but that same day all exits from the Devil's Cauldron presented mixed climbing of the greatest difficulty. In a previous winter, of early February 1977, the position was reversed with the '100 ft Wall' being extremely difficult under thin ice, while the Devil's Cauldron was unrecognisable under a great snow bed. Earlier still, in late March 1974, all 16 pitches carried ice and a strong party took 10 hours to complete the route. Even in summer, conditions can be more akin to an Alpine route than a Scottish rock climb and in June 1977 a huge bed of névé obliterated the lower two of the 'Triple Chimneys' and was only overcome by step-cutting with a peg-hammer and a spectacular leap across a bergschrund. Whatever conditions might appear to be from the Glen Etive road, those approaching the Chasm in winter should always be prepared for a route of Grade V.

Easy Ascents on Stob Dearg

Coire na Tulaich, almost due south of Lagangarbh Cottage presents the most straightforward summer route to the summit ridge of Buachaille Etive Mór, from where bouldery slopes lead east to the top. From Glen Etive an ascent can be made to the same dip on the summit ridge by way of Coire Cloiche Finne, but this rough corrie is more often used as an involuntary descent in the confusing conditions that can reign in bad weather, or in winter by those deterred from descending over the cornice that often forms at the head of Coire na Tulaich. In descent this crucial bealach (870 m) between the two corries will be found in poor visibility on a course from the summit cairn of 258° for 200 m and then 280° for 300 m. It should be stressed that in the wild conditions that can prevail on any winter's day, holding such a meticulous compass course is not easy and that unless the bealach is positively identified and a clear view be had down the steep snow slope at the head of Coire na Tulaich, it is safer to turn down south into Coire Cloiche Finne.

Stob Dearg with its challenging front and its splendid view across the expanse of Rannoch Moor is only a part of Buachaille Etive Mór, which twists as a ridge over three other tops in a south-westerly direction, and makes a fine high-level walk. If ascent has been made via Coire na Tulaich, a traverse of the ridge and return by the deep glen to the west, Lairig Gartain, is not too long a day. Individually the tops of **Stob na Doire** (1011 m), **Stob Coire Altruim** (939 m) and **Stob na Broige** (956 m) can each be ascended without difficulty from Glen Etive and the latter top gives a particularly fine view down the glen to the loch. Stob Coire Altruim has a north-east facing buttress of perhaps 100 m height almost beneath its summit cloven by a deeply recessed gully that makes a pleasant winter climb at Grade II. It was first climbed by T. Graham Brown and J. G. Parish in February 1950.

Buachaille Etive Beag—Stob Dubh (958 m)

Like its larger companion across the Lairig Gartain, this hill presents a bold face to the main road, but here the similarity ends as there is insufficient continuous rock for worthwhile climbing on the north-eastern face of Stob nan Cabar (776 m) and, the highest top, Stob Dubh, lies hidden at the south-western point of the main ridge. Very much overshadowed by its grander neighbours, Buachaille Etive Beag is nevertheless mountainous and the only open, easy slopes lie to the north-west. Most descents are made into the Lairig Gartain and, particularly from Stob nan Cabar (the top of the rafters), an easterly descent on a winter's evening—perhaps after a traverse of Buachaille Etive Mór and Buachaille Etive Beag—requires a lot of care. This slope is cut by a series of gullies, well shown on the O.S. 1:50,000 map, Sheet 41, all of which contain rock pitches: the second counting from the north forks and the left fork contains sufficient rock-climbing to make an interesting route to the summit ridge. It was first climbed by J. G. Parish, T. Graham Brown, E. W. Scott and G. S. Brown in June 1950 and some of the pitches are Difficult.

Bidean nam Bian (1150 m)

While Buachaille Etive Mór stands guard on the 'wrong' side of the breached headwall of Glencoe, Bidean nam Bian sits majesti-cally on its throne and splays its feet onto the very floor of the glen. From all sides its appearance is grand and mountainous but its complexity is such that only repeated visits bring appreciation of its form. Its main ridge forms a north-facing arc which, from its centre projects another 'Y'-shaped ridge—An t'Sron and Beinn Fhada are the western and eastern outposts of the main ridge and Stob Coire nan Lochan with its own northern ridges of Aonach Dubh and Geàrr Anoach, makes up the central prong. A traverse in summer from Aonach Dubh by way of *Dinnertime Buttress*, over all the tops to Beinn Fhada, with a descent into the 'Lost Valley' (Coire Gabhail) is one of the finest outings in

89

the British Isles and is open to hill-goers with only modest mountaineering experience—it is of course much more demanding in winter. 'Dinnertime Buttress' lies on the west face of Aonach Dubh which is pleated by a series of gullies and slim buttresses—well seen from the road near the Clachaig Hotel—and is the left-most of the buttresses underneath the shallow bealach north of Aonach Dubh. It is easily reached by crossing the burn below the waterfall at about the 200 m level. The only rock encountered on it is 50 m of moderate scrambling near the top and this can be avoided by traversing right into No. 2 Gully.

A simple ascent into Coire Gabhail is an enchanting experience, the approach having the aura of that of an Alpine peak with paths clinging to steep slopes and a jungle of boulders and trees hiding, until the last moment, the awesome view of the cirque of jagged tops and steep walls that enclose the alluvial flats. This remarkable feature, and much of the maze beneath it, resulted from an enormous landslide from the western slope of Beinn Fhada, behind which a lake formed to eventually wash away its retaining wall and leave exposed its flat bed of shingle. Autumn, with a golden glow from the birches in the gorge at the head of the glen and perhaps an early snow-fall to add to the majesty of the peaks, is a particularly repaying season for a visit.

For ascent of Bidean nam Bian itself, the most straightforward approach is from the west end of Loch Achtriochtan. A steep path climbs on the west side of the waterfall up to the lip of the corrie and skirts the eastern slope of An t'Sron where a little scrambling is required. Where the burn divides the path crosses to follow the west side of the easternmost fork, though it now becomes faint. The burn can be followed up to a tiny lochan, above which steep scree leads to the bealach between Bidean nam Bian and Stob Coire nan Lochan. Either peak can be ascended easily from this bealach, but if descending toward it from Bidean, great care is needed in poor visibility as the natural trend of the ground carries one out onto the top of Diamond Buttress. These bare details do no justice to the magnificence of Coire nam Beithach surrounded by steep crags which unfold slowly on the right as one ascends, until towering above are the huge buttresses of the Diamond on the left and Church Door on the right, divided by the Central Gully. Little wonder that the early mountaineers rejoiced at being able to rise from their breakfast table in the Clachaig Hotel and wander up to try new routes in this Alpine cirque. The main lodestone soon became the Church Door Buttress, probably through Norman Collie who during a fortnight in March 1894 made first ascents with Solly, Collier and Hastings of Tower Ridge, his own climb on Buachaille Etive Mór and one of the buttresses of Stob Coire nam Beith (not recorded but probably No. 4), and whose unfailing eye for a feasible mountain route would have sought out the weakness in the massive structure of the Church Door. Thereafter between 1895 and 1898, Tough and Brown came down from Aberdeen; Hastings, Haskett-Smith and Bowen came up from the far south; and Raeburn and J. H. Bell led successive forays from Glasgow and Edinburgh. In all six attempts were made, usually in rain or snow, before Raeburn and Bell led the seventh and successful assault with R. G. Napier and H. C. Boyd. Their fascination with the buttress and with the obscure line of weakness that they followed, known now as the 'Flake Route', is understandable. Above the pinnacle (Collie's Pinnacle) that plugs the base of the Central Gully, there lies hidden a great split in the buttresss that allows one to 'chimney' up to a platform. Then when it appears that progress can only be made by a traverse out onto the very steep face, another hidden line of weakness slants upwards and left above 'The Arch' formed by two, enormous boulders jammed across the vertical wall. As one traverses comfortably across one can peer down vertically through a gap to the scree 60 m below: above, the climbing is merely steep and difficult.

Apart from the generally hard rock-climbing on the Diamond and Church Door Buttresses, Coire nam Beithach provides great scope for general mountaineering. Four buttresses of rough, clean rhyolite all offer easy scrambling routes converging on the summit of Stob Coire nam Beith while to the right an easily identified, acute triangle of pink rock named the 'Pyramid' offers an introduction to difficult climbing. The rock is clean, rough and sound, though near the top there is a detached flake resting on a good foundation that needs careful handling. Under snow and ice the four numbered buttresses offer a good introduction to the middle grade of winter climbing and they are split by chimneys and gullies containing harder and classic routes. K. V. Crocket's selective guide contains the best routes and two very clear diagrams of the major crags—a necessity as the topography of Stob Coire nam Beiths' buttresses is complex.

An-t-Sron (850 m), whose 'Chasm' so apparent from the main road marks the eroded line of the ancient ring-fracture, can be climbed directly from the main road and, while the initial 700 m are tiresomely steep, there follows a fine ridge-walk of 2 km over the tops of Stob Coire nam Beith. That part of the ridge between Stob Coire nam Beith and Bidean often carries in winter a delicate snow arête.

Another ascent of Bidean nam Bian, not an obvious approach and only recommended for winter, is by the vast south face. When stable snow conditions exist on this face its sunny exposure and complexity of ribs and couloirs give easy mountaineering in a delightful, Alpine atmosphere. It can be reached best by following the Fionn Ghleann to the bealach between Bidean and Beinn Maol Chaluim, as the southern approach up Gleann Fhaolain from Glen Etive involves a struggle through afforestation. However the burn in the Fionn Ghleann takes enormous drainage and can run its straight course with awesome force—fortunately there is no need to ford it and its west bank can be reached around the nose of Aonach Dubh a'Ghlinne from the farm of Gleann-leac-na-muidhe.

There have appeared lighthearted accounts of descents made on this side of the hill in error, but while picking a line to suit one's taste on a sunny, winter's morning is a straightforward affair, these slopes and those above the Fionn Ghleann are no place to descend on a winter's evening.

Stob Coire nan Lochan (1115 m)

The winter view of this peak from points above the main road and near the Meeting of the Three Waters, is one of the splendours of Glencoe: higher up, at the lowest point between Gearr Aonach and the peak itself, there is an uninterrupted view of the vertical pillars and deeply recessed gullies that line the east face of the north ridge. Perhaps the most interesting approach leads along the crest of Geàrr Aonach, reached from the mouth of Coire Gabhail by the 'Zig-Zags'. This path winds through the most unlikely terrain and uses a series of ledges on the steep, north-eastern nose with a little scrambling in between. Its base is easily enough found—at the left end of the fourth terrace up

from the burn under steep rock—but in descent careful prospect-
ing will be needed before the top is identified: it will be found in
the area between the northernmost of the steep gullies that drop
to the east and the final steep nose that plummets into Glencoe,
but many false casts have left misleading traces. Under snow and
with no recent tracks those without previous knowledge could
spend considerable time searching for this descent. It should be
emphasised that the 'Zig-Zags' is the only easy scrambling route
onto and off Geàrr Aonach until one reaches the shallow
depression at the south-west of the ridge before the rise onto
Stob Coire nam Lochan. There is good rock climbing on both
the north-east and the east face of Geàrr Aonach and high on the
latter face some excellent winter routes that need a hard winter
(see K. V. Crocket's *Selective Guide*). The south-eastern aspect
making for pleasant rock-climbing conditions on this east face,
can in winter bring very dangerous ice and stone-fall—some
huge, Damoclean icicles have been seen to fall from the upper
walls when early morning frost prevailed lower down.

Two valley approaches, other than that by Coire nam Beithach,
are regular routes to Stob Coire nan Lochan: that by Coire
Gabhail has a path on the west side of the glen starting beyond
the flats and near the point where the substantial burn disappears
underground not to reappear until beneath the debris of the
great land-slip. The path carries up to the gorge, but the ground
above to the bealach between the peak and Bidean nam Bian is
rough going. Also, in winter this slope holds much snow, as does
the whole head-wall of this glen, and is prone to avalanche.

The glen to the west leading to Coire nan Lochan has just as
much scenic interest in the burn tumbling through the rocky
gorge and higher in the spread of lochans beneath the columnar
crags: easy ground can be followed from these lochans either
east to gain the north-east ridge or north-west to gain the north
ridge. The former ridge has steep sections of shattered rock that
require care. A good path runs up the east side of the glen giving
good views of the rock-climbing playground on the east face of
Aonach Dubh and carries beyond the 600 m level before fading
at the rock barrier beneath the lip of the corrie: it makes the
ideal approach for those planning to climb some of the classic
winter routes. One of the gullies, 'Broad Gully', seen from the
corrie bed as the leftmost in the mural, makes an easy winter

route to the summit and in good snow conditions a steep glissade.

Both Coire Gabhail and Coire nan Lochan are easily reached opposite their entrances, by bridges crossing the River Coe.

Much has been written about 'Ossian's Cave', the black cleft so obvious high on the north face of Aonach Dubh. It used to contain a metal box for calling cards but this interesting relic vanished some years ago and there remains nothing else to recommend about what is always a vegetatious and usually wet scramble with no view and with an inelegant, seated shuffle offering the only security in descent. There have been several accidents to parties descending from the Cave.

Stob Coire Sgreamhach (1072 m), Beinn Fhada (952 m), Beinn Maol Chaluim (907 m)

These two outliers of Bidean nam Bian form the jagged outline at the head of the 'Lost Valley' and only from Glen Etive can easy slopes be found on the southern flank of Stob Coire Sgreamhach. When they feature as the last tops in a traverse from Stob Coire nan Lochan, they provide a sting in the tail, for there are awkward, descending steps beyond Stob Coire Sgreamhach—always best turned on the right—and the multiple tops on Beinn Fhada (truly the long hill as the Gaelic translates) seem more than their number. Purists who wish to keep high until the final nose of Beinn Fhada can scramble down the vegetatious shelf that lies east of the nose but careful route-finding in daylight are prerequisites for a comfortable descent here. There is a footbridge across the Allt Coire Gabhail at 174563 not shown on the O.S. 1:50,000 Second Series map, Sheet 41.

Otherwise the only straightforward descent from Beinn Fhada is into Coire Gabhail taking the first gully beyond, i.e. north of, the last top of 823 m and keeping to the slope left (south) of the gully. This gully leads down onto the alluvial flats beside an enormous boulder that offers some well-polished problems.

From Glen Etive, starting up the forest edge near Dalness, a most enjoyable traverse can be made of Stob Coire Sgreamhach, Bidean nam Bian and Beinn Maol Chaluin (907 m). When no snow lies the contrast between the various rock-types is remarkable with the quartzite boulder field capping Beinn Maol Chaluin particularly noticeable—it gives some idea of the enormous forces that went to provide the underlying structure of the area, to realise that an immense folding movement in the Earth's crust superimposed this quartzite on the younger Leven schist that makes up the bulk of the hill. Also, in early summer the southern spur of this peak, as it slopes down into Glen Etive, displays a rich crop of wild orchid, variegated in colour from the palest of pinks to purple.

In winter much interest can be added to this traverse by climbing the 'Sron na Lairig', a Grade II route that follows the ridge bounding the southern rim of Stob Coire Sgreamhach's eastern corrie. This winter climb is usually approached from the north via the Lairig Eilde but the southern approach on the path from Dalness leads through an impressive gorge and reserves sight of the route until the bealach at 490 m. (The path continues through the Lairig Eilde to the Glencoe road. It fords the burn twice and that nearest the main road can be a complete barrier after heavy rain.)

If icy conditions have been found in the first half of this traverse, the descent of Bidean nam Bian to the Bealach Fhaolain (not marked on the 1 : 50,000 map: lies due north of Beinn Maol Chaluim) should be treated with respect. There is a dog-leg course of 1 km due west then south that hinges on the steepest part of a convex slope which commences at a deceptively easy angle.

Beinn Maol Chaluim is a fine, mountainous peak in its own right with very steep flanks to either side of its north-south spine, and with a crag, Creag Dubh, of schist frowning down upon the Bealach Fhionnghaill. This crag of perhaps 100 m height, is unusually compact for schist and may well repay exploration. From the Bealach Fhionnghaill a path skirting left around the base of the crag, and leading eventually past other smaller outcrops of porphyry, offers the only easy, though circuitous route to the summit. In hard winters a deeply recessed gully on the eastern flank beneath the southern top (848 m) makes an enjoyable climb at Grade II.

Accommodation

See pages 81 and 101.

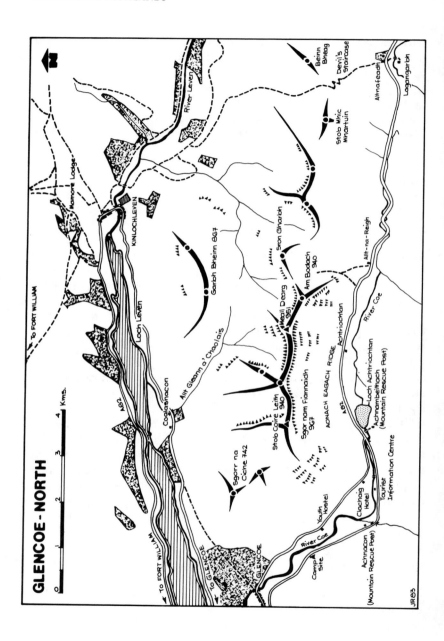

GLENCOE - NORTH

7

Glencoe North and Rannoch Moor

Aonach Eagach
Am Bodach (943 m)
*****Meall Dearg** (953 m)
Stob Coire Leith (940 m)
*****Sgòr nam Fiannaidh** (967 m)
Sgòr na Ciche (742 m)
Garbh Bheinn (867 m)

From the constricted depths of Glencoe the splendour of Aonach Eagach's airy crest is not well appreciated and only those who traverse its jagged pinnacles will realise how slender the ridge is. To enjoy this outing one should ideally have some rock-climbing experience and those without would probably better maintain their composure if a rope were used for short sections. In true winter conditions that part between Am Bodach and Stob Coire Leith can be very difficult indeed and the bare standard given of Grade III is not truly indicative of the variety of problems nor of the scale. Such extreme conditions are uncommon but any party venturing onto the ridge on one of the shorter winter days would do well to start early and to keep moving. Frequently, experienced parties have had a casual attitude on a fine winter's day repaid with a struggle to find a safe descent in darkness.

Most parties carry out the traverse from east to west and this direction offers a saving of 150 m of ascent onto Am Bodach and, in summer, the easiest way of tackling the awkward sections. The south-south-east ridge of Am Bodach can be ascended directly from the cottage of Allt-na-ruigh, or a path can be followed into the ravine east of the ridge. From the top of Am Bodach the easiest line of descent west onto the ridge is not obvious but a cast to the right should succeed. A little north of the next top, Meall Dearg, lies a great boulder of rough and creamy granite carried there by the vast ice-sheet that once covered Rannoch Moor and all the surrounding hills—it was evidently over 700 m thick. Meall Dearg is the site of another curiosity, for it was the last Munro of the first of that exclusive band to have climbed all those Scottish hills designated by Sir Hugh Munro as having a separate status of more than 3000 ft. The Reverend A. E. Robertson, for he it was, endeared himself to future Munroists by kissing first the cairn and then his wife.

Between Meall Dearg and Stob Coire Leith, though the ridge twists and undulates, the route is obvious and involves most pleasantly varied scrambling, the highlight of which is a particularly narrow section turreted with two crazy pinnacles: these should be clambered over directly as circumvention to the right involves loose rock and vegetation. After Stob Coire Leith the ridge broadens and near the top of Sgòr nam Fiannaidh boulders of quartzite appear underfoot. For those wishing to descend directly into Glencoe the open corrie south of Sgòr nam Fiannaidh offers better going in summer than the unpleasant and dangerous path that hugs the western rim of Clachaig Gully. In places this path has been worn down to the underlying rock, it approaches very close to the lip of the gully where long strips of turf have been undermined, and in wet weather it makes a thoroughly nasty descent. A more comfortable descent will be found by following the ridge from Sgòr nam Fiannaidh west and then west-north-west onto the open, heathery slopes above the old road.

There is no easy summer descent to the south between Am Bodach and Stob Coire Leith and, in winter this caution should be extended to include the corrie above Loch Achtriochtan and also that above the cottage of Allt-na-Ruigh, both being potential avalanche sites. If a party suspects dangerous snow conditions it is far safer to continue to the bealach between Sgòr nam Fiannaidh and Sgòr na Ciche or, at the eastern end, to face the steepness of the south-south-east ridge of Am Bodach. There are easy descents north from both Meall Dearg and Stob Coire Leith but these would be desperate measures indeed for a party returning to Glencoe.

Climbs have been made, winter and summer, on the south-western aspect of Am Bodach and some are described in K. V.

45.   *Looking out of Clachaig Gully on a fine June day.*   *Peter Hodgkiss*

46.   *Clachaig Gully: The Red Chimney—pleasant climbing.*   *Peter Hodgkiss*

47.   *Not so pleasant!*   *Peter Hodgkiss*

48.   *Aonach Eagach from the east.*   *Peter Hodgkiss*

49. *Aonach Eagach from the west with a great cloud-sea covering Rannoch Moor.*
Peter Hodgkiss

50. *Scrambling over the pinnacles between Meall Dearg and Stob Coire Leith.*

Peter Hodgkiss

51. *Approaching Binnein Mór's summit from the north.* *Peter Hodgkiss*

52 and 53. *The Blackwater Dam under construction in 1905 and 1906. The outline of Buachaille Etive Mór is clear in the background.*
54. *Corrour Lodge before the First World War looking stark without its eventual screen of trees. The building was destroyed by fire in the 1930's (reproduced by courtesy of the Curator, Pollok House and D. Maxwell MacDonald).*

Crocket's selective guide, but the route worthy of real note on the north side of the glen is the 'Clachaig Gully'—an expedition of character containing some fine pitches. Cleaving the hillside so obviously above the Clachaig Hotel it did not escape the attention of the pioneers and Collie, with Solly and Collier, was the first to make an attempt. Nor surprisingly, the month being March (1894), they were turned back by a cascade pouring over the 'Great-Cave' (pitch 4). What does cause surprise is that men of such ability as Raeburn and later, J. H. B. Bell, with their predilection for difficult gullies and their preparedness to tackle loose and vegetated rock, should have left it unclimbed until W. H. Murray, A. M. MacAlpine, J. K. W. Dunn and W. G. Marskell made the first ascent in May 1938.

Facing only a little west of south the climbing can be on sun-warmed rock and, unlike most gullies, a dry spell will remove most of the drainage water, but leaving always Jericho Wall greasy from seepage. Above the 'Great Cave' escape routes are as difficult as the climbing in the gully above and, even lower, they are unattractively vegetated and steep. With a good flow of water coursing down the gully it is an awesome place but the major waterfalls are turned on their right walls and only the 'Red Chimney' must be climbed direct.

Sgòr na Ciche (742 m)

This prominent cone usually known as the Pap of Glencoe, offers a fine viewpoint for an evening's walk. A good path leads up the hill almost 1 km east of Bridge of Coe on the old road. It runs up to the bealach between the Pap and Sgòr nam Fiannaidh and can be followed up the steep, southern slope to the top. A little west of the summit smooth slabs of quartzite are scored with south-westerly directed striae—the parallel furrows ground out by glaciation—and further down the slope (at the 250 m level; NN 115586), ancient man has left his mark in a series of trenches thought to have been dug by Fingal's horde as fortification against the Norse invaders.

Eastern end

Stob Mhic Mhartuin (706 m) to Sron Gharbh (873 m)

These two hills, separated by two other unnamed tops, form the

continuation of the Aonach Eagach, with the ridge between Am
Bodach and Sron Gharbh falling only to a bealach at 816 m.
They make a fitting start, or finish, to a traverse of the Aonach
Eagach and in themselves offer an easy afternoon's exercise
from Altnafeadh. Views from them are out of proportion to
their relatively minor status and a sense of perspective is gained
of the Bidean range and of its corries that is lost from the
confusing proximity of the Aonach Eagach itself. Below the
most westerly of the two unnamed tops lies a prominent point
known as A'Chailleach (the old woman) with, as is usual with
Gaelic nomenclature of hill form, Am Bodach (the old man)
across the corrie. On the south-eastern slope of A' Chailleach a
rarely climbed gully, Red Funnel Gully, offers a taste of exploration: it starts at approximately 500 m and though the lower
pitches are merely scrambling, there are two long pitches in the
upper half that are Very Difficult. The gully was first climbed by
J. G. Parish, T. Graham Brown and R. Fox in 1950.

Garbh Bheinn (867 m)

Despite its proximity to Kinlochleven, this hill gives a decided
sense of remoteness. Its northern flank is steep and rugged while
to the south it is walled in by the Aonach Eagach. It was
on Garbh Bheinn that Robert Louis Stevenson, in his novel
Kidnapped, had David Balfour lie nursing his hunger while Alan
Breac brought food up from Caolasnacon. The easiest approach
is by the track on the south bank of the River Leven that
turns south up to the reservoir supplying domestic water to
Kinlochleven: above easy slopes lead to a plateau east of the top.
From the farm at Caolasnacon a fine circuit can be made over
the knolls on the west ridge and then, via the bealach (530 m) to
the south, on to traverse the Aonach Eagach and Sgòr na Ciche.

Until 1922 and the completion of the road along the
southern shore of Loch Leven—started with the labour of
German prisoners of war—all transport from the south reached
Kinlochleven by boat, and the narrows at Caolasnacon (meaning in Gaelic 'the narrows of Con') needed dredging and the
diversion of the silt-carrying Allt Gleann a' Chaolais before a
passenger boat of any size could be used. These narrows were
not cleared until 1907 and, before then the motor-boats in use,

often with rowing-boats for extra passengers in tow, could only overcome the full tidal force when empty; so that all passengers were put off at one end of the channel and had to cross the swampy flats to the other end carrying their rowing boat with them.

Accommodation

This area is very well served by accommodation of all types. There are camp-sites at Invercoe, Leacantuim, Caolasnacon and the Caravan Club site 2 km south of Glencoe village which is hidden from view above and west of the main road. On the old road there is the Youth Hostel and the Clachaig Hotel which has a bunkhouse open all the year round and in Glencoe village there is another hotel and several bed and breakfast houses (Glencoe Tourist Office—telephone 08552 296). At the eastern end of the glen there is the SMC hut at Lagangarbh available to members of affiliated clubs (and as mentioned in the previous chapter, the hut of the Ladies Scottish Climbing Club, and the Kingshouse Hotel with its bunkhouse).

References

SMCJ, IX, p. 135. Article by J. H. Bell on the early attempts on Church Door Buttress.
SMCJ, XXII, p. 116. *The Geology of Glencoe*, E. B. Bailey.
Always a Little Further, Alastair Borthwick. For a vivid account of an ascent of the Chasm.
Mountaineering in Scotland, and Undiscovered Scotland, W. H. Murray. A compendium, (Diadem 1982), containing classic accounts of first ascents in Glencoe.

Rannoch Moor

This moor represents a vast basin scoured out of granite 400 million years old by successive periods of glaciation and now covered by blanket bog broken by an extended waterway draining from the north-east corner. It is hemmed in on all sides by high hills made of rocks more resistant to the forces of glaciation and takes the shape of an inverted triangle having a base made by the high ground running from Beinn a' Chrulaiste

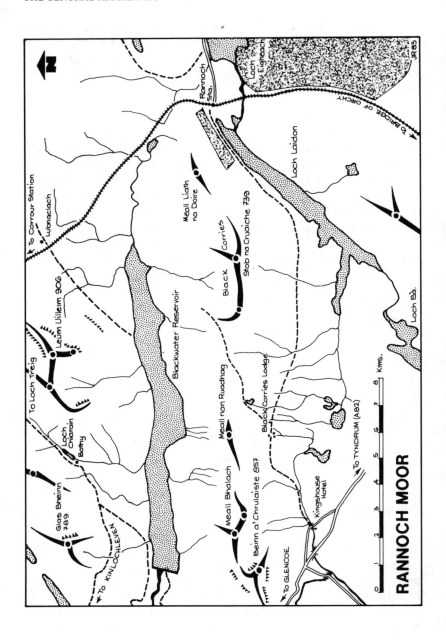

RANNOCH MOOR

to Rannoch Station and sides composed of the railway line and the A82 road.

Bare physical details however, give little impression of the scenic quality which is perhaps best appreciated in descent from one of the easterly ridges on the Black Mount, from where the great channel winding and stretching from Ba Bridge to Loch Laidon adds greatly to the sense of scale. This same sense of space is to be experienced when crossing the moor—an outing to be reserved for clear weather with dry conditions underfoot, or alternatively, a hard frost in winter. Then the expanse of the moor with its scattering of lochans, knolls, and granite boulders, is accentuated by the distant circle of peaks rising abruptly at the moor's edge.

A crossing can be made with relative ease by the track between the Kingshouse Hotel and Rannoch Station, with only a 3 km stretch west of the ruined croft at Tigh na Cruaiche where the track degenerates into rough going. But to experience a real sense of remoteness, the line of Loch Laidon and Loch Bà should be followed. Then the flatness of the moor can be appreciated—in 21 km from Bà Bridge to the northern and of Loch Laidon there is a drop of only 44 m—though an hour of leaping from one tussock to another can make steep ground seem easy going. Following the waterway by canoe has become a popular expedition and, in hard winters, the same route has been followed on skates.

Beinn a' Chrulaiste (857 m), Meall nan Ruadhag (646 m), Stob na Cruaiche (739 m)

To walk this stretch of high ground between the Blackwater and Rannoch Moor gives a taste of remoteness without the heavy going that a crossing of the moor entails. Starting from the Kingshouse Beinn a Chrulaiste is easily ascended by its east ridge and in return it is worth holding due west from Stob na Cruaiche until the path (clearly shown on the 1:50,000 but not on the One Inch to One Mile O.S. maps) is found leading from the Black Corries north of the Stob, down to the lodge of the same name, (though local people know this group of buildings as the Iron Lodge).

Before the opening of the West Highland Railway and when

103

the Blackwater was a mere scatter of lochans, a drove route crossed these hills taking the lairig between Meall a Bhalach and Meall nan Ruadhag. Until a century ago thousands of cattle and sheep crossed this pass each year but it wants an optimistic eye to find any trace now beside the Allt Chailleach on the south and the Allt nan Fuaran to the north. Further north a path on the east side of the Ciaran Water can be followed almost into the Blackwater and, before the inundation of 1906, led to the stance at Ciaran between Lochan Inbhir and Lochan na-Salach-Uidhre.

The Blackwater Hills

Leum Uilleam (906 m), Glas Bheinn (789 m)

These two hills are divided by the course of the old drove road from Lochtreighead to the Ciaran Water and there is still a good path that can be followed down the Allt an Inbhir to the damhead and on to Kinlochleven. Further tracks encircle the northern arc about this area but despite such easy access promoted further by the presence of Corrour Station at c. 400 m close under the north-eastern corrie of Leum Uilleam, the hills are rarely visited.

To ascend Glas Bheinn from Kinlochleven a good path can be followed on the north side of the River Leven, past the site of the prisoner-of-war camp where German soldiers were kept during the First World War, to the dam head. Those travelling across country from the north will find the most gentle ascent on Glass Bheinn's north-north-east spine, where 2 km of ridge rise by a mere 30 m, allowing one to walk hands-in-pockets and enjoy the fine views to the west.

No more than 2 hours is needed for the easy walk up Leum Uilleam from Corrour Station. The central, indeed almost pivotal position of this top within a great, northern arc of higher hills makes it a grand viewpoint. It holds more snow than its height might suggest.

A path skirts the south-eastern flank of Leum Uilleam from the house at Lubnaclach, but like that beside the Ciaran Water, it runs into the Blackwater. Beyond to the west the shore of the reservoir offers very rough going only exceeded by that on the opposite shore.

Accommodation

Apart from the existence of the hotel at Rannoch Station, the Blackwater Hills and, to a lesser extent, Rannoch Moor is the country of the bothies. There are four small bothies maintained by the Mountain Bothies Association and offering simple shelter, but their spirit is best appreciated by parties of two or less who can happily contemplate the arrival of another such party.

In the south Gortan is easily reached by the track beside the Water of Tulla but continuation north has been made difficult with the recent planting of conifers on both sides of the railway line, although a good track can be followed beside the railway to the 'Soldiers' Trenches' where it cuts under the line and turns east into Gleann Chomraidh. North of the Blackwater, Ciaran bothy lies beside the loch of the same name and the house was built to replace that now under the waters of the reservoir; while further north Staoineag and Meanach lie not 4 km apart on the Amhainn Rath. The latter is not shown on O.S. maps: it sits opposite Luibeilt on the north shore of the burn, which, both here and at Staoineag, can be difficult to ford.

References

Blackwood's Magazine; Sept. 1927. Article—*Benighted on the Moor of Rannoch* (reprinted in SMCJ, XXI, pp. 29 and 165).

Children of the Dead End. Pat McGill (Caliban 1982). A vivid novel centering round the life of the itinerant workers during the construction of the Blackwater Dam.

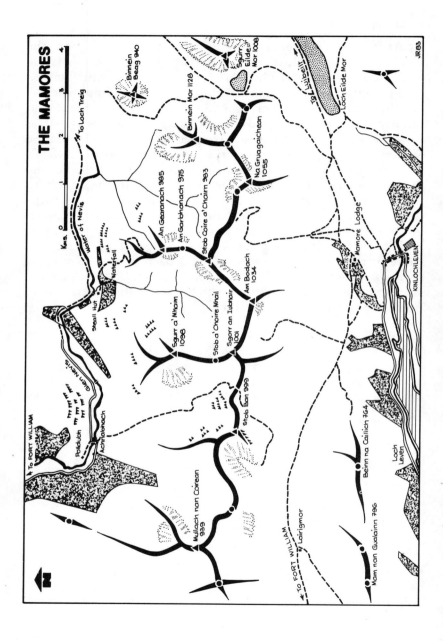

*Sgurr Eilde Mor (1008 m)
*Binnein Beag (940 m)
*Binnein Mor (1128 m)
*Na Gruagaichean (1055 m)
  North-west top (1036 m)
*An Gearanach (982 m)
 An Garbhanach (975 m)
*Stop Coire a' Chairn (981 m)
*Am Bodach (1032 m)
*Sgor an Iubhair (1001 m)
*Sgurr a' Mhaim (1099 m)
*Stob Ban (999 m)
*Mullach nam Coirean (939 m)

A gently rising and extensive moor of great size—as might be the
meaning of the name 'Mamore'—seems hardly appropriate to
this mountainous ridge stretching some 20 kms east to west and
throwing out ribs north and south that, even from the valley, are
obviously steep and sharp. To walk the length of the ridge in a
day makes a splendid outing—long certainly but with only
occasional difficulties to interrupt a steady pace. Kinlochleven
makes the most convenient starting point with the estate road to
Loch Eilde Mor and the old military road to Fort William
providing easy going for the first two hours and for the last, long
hour. As three of the main tops are removed from the ridge on
northern spurs, the distance for the round trip is greater at
c. 33 km than a casual glance at the O.S. map might suggest;
however the main ridge does not drop below 745 m, and in a
westerly traverse, reserves its gentlest slopes until the last top. If
the eastern outliers of Binnein Beag and Sgurr Eilde Mor are
included, the additional 8 km or so, with the extra ascent, make
the traverse a very long outing and one that on a short winter's
day will be started and finished in darkness.

Sgurr Eilde Mór (1008 m)

From Kinlochleven a good path crosses the burn draining from the east past the north end of the village and ascends in a northerly direction to connect at c. 300 m with the land-rover track running east along the north side of Loch Eilde Mór. (Another path strikes more directly east to a fine waterfall and continues steeply up a spur between a bifurcation of the burn, but higher this path dwindles and it is probably as quick to follow the dog-leg of the first-mentioned.) A stalker's path winds north-east to the lochan beneath Sgurr Eilde Mór's south-western flank which is best ascended to the right. The spine of the hill runs for 2 km in a northerly direction and is paved with distinctive platelets of schist broken by outcroppings of quartz. Here and there are gravelly clearings and, particularly on the western flank, occasional clumps of moss campion can be found in flower from June to August.

Binnein Beag (940 m)

The path system described under Sgurr Eilde Mor offers the easiest approach to this hill and, from the lochan at 730 m, the path continues further north across the eastern flank of Binnein Mor than is shown on the O.S. 1:50,000 map. Rough scree slopes encircle the hill and seem at their longest in the northern arc. Such bad footing do they make that it is worthwhile, in approach from Glen Nevis, bearing for the bealach between Binnein Beag and Mor. In its somewhat isolated position above Glen Nevis, the hill makes a fine viewpoint with the huge bulk of Ben Nevis and the sharp outline of its North east Buttress particularly impressive; nearer at hand the slender north-east ridge of Binnein Mór is an attractive prospect.

Binnein Mór (1128 m)

For such a large hill Binnein Mór is not a conspicuous distant feature, although the regular shape of its north-eastern corrie is distinctive from the east. Whilst there are no recognised climbs, the northern ridges offer sporting ascents and, with little exception, the slopes on all sides are very steep. The summit ridge runs north-south and has appendages giving on a map rather the shape of an 'X'. A straightforward route via the south-eastern wing uses again the path system described under Sgurr Eilde Mór and the stalker's path leading into Coire an Lochain should be followed to c. 730 m where well-engineered zig-zags carry one directly north to the top known rather confusingly to those who climb hills rather than look at them, as Sgurr Eilde Beag. In winter the ridge ahead is often beautifully corniced and leads easily over a southern top to the final sharp point.

For a traverse of the hill, the north-east ridge makes a most enjoyable scramble exiting steeply onto the summit ridge just north of the cairn, but its winter ascent demands care. At an easier angle is the north-north-west ridge which is an obvious approach from Glen Nevis: in most winters this ridge carries much snow which tends to form an arête of shallow but regular curvature which is a fine thing to look upon. The last wing of Binnein Mor carries the main ridge south east to Na Gruagaichean.

Na Gruagaichean (1055 m)

Few hills of comparable stature can be so little climbed in their own right. Lying so close between the obvious attractions of the ridges thrust out north by Binnein Mór and An Garbhanach, its grace of form, and the complexity of its twin tops, is only revealed when approaching along the main ridge; and, the winter view of the north-west top from the neck between the two peaks is breathtaking in the juxtaposition of the very steep, eastern slope in the foreground against the Alpine grace of the distant Carn Mór Dearg. Both slopes down into the neck require care in icy conditions and neither the easy slopes to east and west nor the drawing of the contours on the O.S. map prepare one for the sharp dip of 70 m.

An Garbhanach (975 m), An Gearanach (982 m)

To approach the mountainous ridge formed by these two peaks from the south by way of Coire na Ba above Mamore Lodge is far less repaying than to start in Glen Nevis, from where the north-facing arc made with Am Bodach and Sgurr a Mhaim makes for a magnificent outing with a strong mountaineering flavour. If they are to be included as part of a traverse of all the Mamore tops, the main ridge must be left at the distinct top of **Stob Coire a Chairn** (981 m), (not named on the O.S. 1:50,000 map).

The path through the Nevis gorge is a delight in itself and it is a sobering thought that but for the efforts of a few individuals at the Public Inquiry in 1961, a hydro-electric scheme might well have inundated this magnificent ravine, described by W. H. Murray as a scene of Himalayan character. Clinging to the northern slopes of the gorge the path winds through mixed woodland of small oak, Scots pine, and birch scrub: it gains little height once into the gorge and runs close enough to the torrent—which is its Gaelic name, Eas an Tuil—for the erosive power of the water to be appreciated.

The Water of Nevis retains its strong flow beyond the meadow flats and is not easily forded, but a wire bridge crosses it at 177685 to Steall Cottage run as a club hut by the Lochaber Mountaineering Club. Within sight and sound of the cottage is the waterfall also known as Steall (st^owl—a deluge, a great quantity of liquid): it has a clear fall of 110 m and is believed to have a greater volume than other, taller falls in Scotland. During long spells of hard frost the fall does freeze, forming marvellous convolutions of ice pillars, between which further pillars can be seen. In these conditions it has been climbed but each account speaks of water running behind the ice and of a disconcerting increase in volume as height is gained. Steall receives enormous drainage from Coire a Mhail and is a fitting outflow from one of the finest hanging valleys in Scotland.

To reach the northern spurs of An Gearanach a path skirts the buttress to the east of the waterfall and turns up south into the fine V-shaped corrie well named Coire Dubh for the frieze of dark rock on its west wall. The path continues up the left side of the burn to about the 400 m level where the glen opens out and where its bed, in late spring, is a mass of blue hyacinth. Above, the burn can be seen descending from a neck and it is probably quicker to strike up rough ground for this point rather than hunting for the easterly windings of the discontinuous path.

Beyond An Gearanach one can wander hands in pockets until the ridge narrows to an arête that demands care in icy conditions.

110

An Gharbhanach falls away to east and west in rocky slopes but there is insufficient continuous rock for climbing.

Am Bodach (1032 m)

This peak is easily reached from the old military road between Mamore Lodge and Fort William, a faint path on the left bank of the burn carrying up to the 750 m level in Coire na h'Eirghe, from where zig-zags continue to the bealach west of the peak. An alternative for descent is the south-south-east ridge which is sharply defined in its upper 100 m but which lower becomes interrupted by shelves of quartzite dipping to the south-west and with awkward and repeated drops from their lips. A line west-south-west from a bump in the ridge at c. 740 m—known as Sgor an Fhuarain—avoids this tiresome ground and leads to the point on the old military road at 172631 where a good path runs down through the indigenous woods to Kinlochleven school.

The peak has an extensive east face which offers winter mountaineering of an easy standard, while steeper, though short lines will be found in the southern sector. Its north ridge is steep enough to be awkward when iced.

Sgurr a' Mhaim (1099 m), Stob a' Choire Mhail (1000 m), Sgorr an Iubhair (1001 m)

This is the longest and most significant arm stretched north from the main ridge. In summer it is an exhilarating scramble but in winter conditions, whether of snow or ice, there are two or three steps along the arête between Stob a' Choire Mhail and the main peak where inexperienced climbers might welcome a rope. (William Inglis Clark when traversing the arête in the summer of 1880, had to lower and raise a nervous companion by his coat collar at the steepish bits. The companion was also handicapped in wearing only smooth-soled leather shoes).

While the three tops can be reached from Kinlochleven by way of the tracks mentioned under Am Bodach, it is far more repaying to approach from Glen Nevis where the splendour of An Steall and Sgurr a' Mhaim's eastern corrie can be appreciated. From Steall Cottage a way can be found up the steep slopes to the west of the waterfall, but without prior knowledge this route is not advised for descent. Once over the lip of the hanging valley, the way to the north-east ridge of Sgurr a' Mhaim is straightforward, but an alternative more in keeping with the expedition is to cross the foot of the eastern corrie, Coire nan Cnamh to scramble up the east ridge. On the back wall of this corrie there is a very clear exposure of folded schist, which can be seen during the approach and, whilst the romantic-sounding name of the corrie has the mundane translation of cud-chewing (cnamh), there is the more romantic inference of cattle driven here for summer pasture (remains of sheilings under the west slope of Stob Coire a' Chairn is evidence of seasonal trans-humanance here).

An obvious continuation of the ridge is to traverse in a great arc over Am Bodach and An Gearanach, though in winter such a day can take much longer than the map distance would indicate. An easier option for return to Glen Nevis, but just as delightful, is to descend the west ridge of Sgorr an Iubhair and then into the glen of Coire a' Mhusgain where an excellent path winds through glacially scoured rocks and lower through indi-genous woodland with fine views of the high crags on either side. For a simple ascent of Sgurr a' Mhaim its north-west ridge provides a straightforward route from Achriabhach in Glen Nevis.

Creag Uamh Shomhairle

Across the Water of Nevis and directly above the car park at the road end in Glen Nevis, this north-westerly facing crag can be reached in 15 minutes. It achieves a maximum height of 100 m, is some 150 yards long and is composed of steep, sound schist. There are currently only three routes on the crag, perhaps due to its sunless and slow-drying aspect when the nearby crags above Polldubh face south and dry out so quickly.

Sunset Boulevard   90 m   Severe
Start near centre of crag at a quartz blaze, right of an overhang and left of a tall light-coloured wall. (1) 18 m. Climb steeply up wall for 5 m on good holds to ledge; traverse left, climb a scoop and move left again to holly tree; chockstone belay. (2) 24 m. Up by crack and wall, past next tree to a groove; climb this to tree

belays. (3) 24 m. Up chimney in corner above; traverse almost horizontally left to grass and trees in overhung bay. (4) 30 m. Up right to corner; piton runner used. Step delicately round on to nose of rib on right, and more delicately into vegetatious chimney; up this to belay. Scrambling remains.

I. Clough, Miss J. Davis, J. Gargett, R. Matthews and D. Ducker,
March 1960.

Sundowner   67 m   Severe
Start on right of crag, at a tree and an arrow. (1) 9 m. Up, trending left, to small stance and belay above overhang. (2) 18 m. To birch tree terrace: delicate last moves. (3) 25 m. Diagonally right, up to steep wall, climb this direct or by a turning movement on right. Either way arrive at sapling. Thence traverse left along ledge and climb groove to flake belay. (4) 15 m. Up slab on right, then straight up wall above; flake belay on left.

I. Clough, Miss J. Davis, J. Gargett, R. Matthews and D. Ducker,
March 1960.

The Strip   96 m   Very Severe
This route lies on the left of the main crag. Start just left of overhanging section about 30 m left of Sunset Boulevard. Climb overhanging crack with aid of inserted nuts to niche with trees (this point may be reached more easily by a diagonal fault from the left) and follow groove to peg belay at holly bush above (20 m). Move awkwardly left (peg runner) and up into groove which follow to ledge below steepening. Go right a few feet and climb vertical dièdre (peg runner). Exit left to gain bay with trees (40 m). Climb rib behind trending left at 14 m then finish straight up to highest point of crag (36 m).

J. Mount and K. Schwartz, August 1971.

Stob Ban (999 m)

From Glen Nevis and particularly from the Pony Track above Achintee, this peak presents a shapely cone, while in certain lights its summit cap of quartzite can look remarkably like snow. However its best aspect is seen from Sgurr a' Mhaim with a north-eastern complex of buttresses and gullies clustered beneath the summit.

The north ridge provides a simple ascent from Polldubh and, once the steep section at mid-height is passed, at an angle easy enough to enjoy the fine views around the compass. From the old military road to the south of Am Bodach the going is much rougher and a pleasanter route can be made my picking up the path between 600 and 700 m and following it north east beneath steep, coggly slopes almost to the bealach, from where the narrow east ridge can be climbed. In the craggy ground south of the east ridge an ice-fall forms in most winters that gives difficult though not serious climbing as escape routes are numerous.

Surprisingly few routes have been made on the crags that stretch across the north-eastern aspect of Stob Ban. They are extensive, steep and offer routes in winter of up to 300 m. Viewed from a little north of east the most prominent feature is a pair of gullies on either side of a broad buttress immediately beneath the summit. The left-hand gully is South Gully and the right-hand one North Gully, but inconsistently the broad buttress has become known as South Buttress. Left of South Gully is a mass of rock named East Wing, while right of North Gully is a slender buttress in the shape of an inverted, acute triangle, known as Central Buttress; to its right a slanting shelf separates Central from North-eastern Buttress. Most of the easy routes have been climbed—South, Central and North-east Buttresses—and whilst the quartzite is not everywhere sound, there is scope for better rock-climbing. In winter there are many attractive routes of a general mountaineering character and some harder lines to be climbed: one such was first ascended by J. Grieve and C. MacNaughton in 1969 when they climbed the left-hand of two prominent chimney/gully systems that seam the east face of the north-east buttress. They assessed the climb at Grade IV, as having a length of 300 m and left it unnamed.

Mullach nan Coirean (939 m)

Suffering by contrast with its more mountainous neighbours to the east, this grassy, easy-angled hill has perhaps the finest views. Its subsidiary top, Meall a' Chaorainn (910 m), has a particularly open view down Loch Linnhe and, from the north ridge of the main top, the steep slopes of Ben Nevis and those of Sgurr a'

55.   *The Mamores from Beinn na Lap. The great crescent-shape of Binnein Mór sits near the centre with the snow cone of Binnein Beag to the right: in between can be seen the distant Sgurr a Mháim.*

Peter Hodgkiss

56. *Na Gruagaichean.*   *Peter Hodgkiss*

57.   *An Gearanach and Sgurr a' Mhaim from Sgurr a' Bhuic.*   *Peter Hodgkiss*

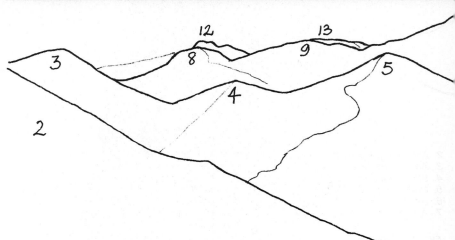

2. Northern slopes of Na Gruagaichean
3. Am Bodach
4. 909 m top
5. Stob Coire a' Chairn
6. An Garbhanach
7. An Gearanach

8. Sgòr an Iubhair
9. Stob Coire a' Mhail
10. Sgùrr a' Mhàim
11. Sròn Coire nan Cnàmh
12. Stob Ban
13. Mullach nan Coirean (part of)

58. From Binnein Mor: that part of Sgurr a' Mhàim known as the "Devil's Ridge" lies between points 9 and 10.   Bert Jenkins

59.   *Sgurr a' Mháim and Stob Bàn over the Carn Mor Dearg Arête.*   *Peter Hodgkiss*

60.   *The C.I.C. hut with the sun behind North-east Buttress.*   *Bert Jenkins*

61.   *The great ridges of Ben Nevis.*   *W. A. Bentall*

Mhaim lend a sense of tremendous scale as they plunge into the rift of Glen Nevis. This north ridge or its parallel north-north-east spur, are easily reached from Achriabhach where a track leads through the afforestation in long zig-zags. At about the 760 m level on the north ridge, just beyond a bump known as Glas Chreag, there is a spring whose waters are cold on the hottest day.

Beinn na Caillich (764 m), Mam na Gualainn (796 m)

These two small hills between Loch Leven and the old military road also provide splendid views, but are more distinguished for bearing a particularly fine stalker's path that maintains a stately progress in well engineered zig-zags to the top of Beinn na Caillich. Rather oddly this path, visible from miles away is not shown on O.S. maps. Local people consider the hill twice wronged by the map-maker as it has always been known by Gaelic speakers as A'Chailleach (the old woman)—as usual across a glen from Am Bodach (the old man).

Long Distance Paths

The route from Fort William through Glen Nevis to Loch Treig —and then beyond either north or west—has been in use for centuries and is considered a right-of-way. It makes a splendid walk in itself apart from providing approach in remote settings to the hills north and south of the glen. The West Highland Line station at Corrour makes the through-route possible inside a day. There are good paths as far as the old and ruined Steall croft in the west and, from Loch Treig to Corrour in the east, but in the central section the track is discontinuous at best and it is well to remember that where the traces cross the Amhainn Rath just east of Luibeilt, the stepping stones are often under 4 ft of water.

For such a flat and boggy place the watershed between the Water of Nevis and the Amhainn Rath is narrow, there being little more than 100 yd between the main water-courses while small tributaries to each are but a few feet apart. Such watersheds have been given the general name of corrom from the Gaelic word cothrom, meaning evenly weighted. The old Gaelic name for this watershed is Moinarmachd, meaning moss of the armour, said to have been derived from the shedding of weapons

E

there by the troops of the Earl of Mar in retreat from the First Battle of Inverlochy.

Accommodation

Steall hut in Glen Nevis—run by the Lochaber M.C. Custodian's address from the Secretary of the Mountaineering Council of Scotland. Youth Hostel in Glen Nevis. Bed and Breakfast accommodation in Kinlochleven where also holiday flats are available at Mamore Lodge on the old military road, telephone 08554 213. Bed and Breakfast and Hotels in Fort William (Tourist Office—Fort William 3581). Bunkhouse accommodation at Achintee Farm, Glen Nevis. Camp-site in Glen Nevis. Manse Barn, Onich—run by the Lomond M.C. Custodian's address from the Secretary of the Mountaineering Council of Scotland. Onich Hut—run by the BMC and MC of S. Contact the Secretary of the Mountaineering Council of Scotland or the BMC at 061-273 5835.

62. *Ben Nevis and Carn Mór Dearg from Binnein Mór* *Gordon Blyth*

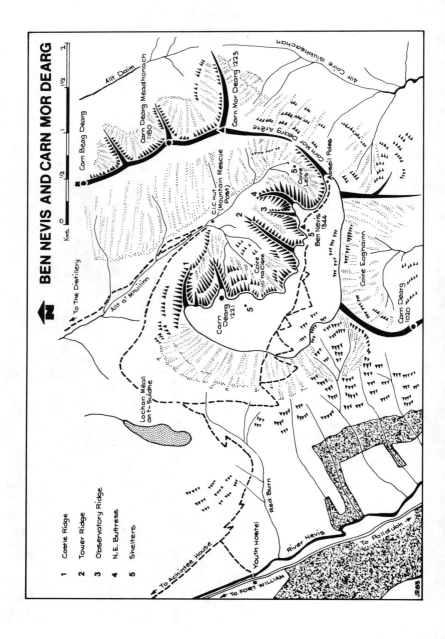

BEN NEVIS AND CARN MOR DEARG

1 Castle Ridge
2 Tower Ridge
3 Observatory Ridge
4 N.E. Buttrees
5 Shelters

9

Ben Nevis
and Carn Mor Dearg

*Ben Nevis (1344 m)
 Carn Dearg
   South-west top (1020 m)
 Carn Dearg
   North west top (1221 m)
*Carn Mor Dearg (1223 m)
 Carn Dearg Mheadhonach (1180 m)

Ben Nevis

Whether seen from the road side or from other hills at great
distance, the height and shape of Ben Nevis is unmistakable.
What is not appreciated from either viewpoint is the detached
nature of the Ben. Its slopes to the west and south plunge into
Glen Nevis, where at Polldubh is produced the longest and
steepest slope in the British Isles–1200 m at an average angle of
over 35°: then the steep slopes to the east and the northern
precipices both drop for 700 m and are interrupted only by the
slender attachment of the Carn Mor Dearg Arête. Most southern
viewpoints do not give a clear impression of the overall steepness
of the Ben and only in a narrow corridor to the west-north-west,
where the pony-track winds its way, does this angle relent.
However from the east and west a proper impression is gained
and the popular viewpoint from Banavie shows the aptness of
Robert Southey's description 'looking as if it had been riven
from the summit to the base, and half of it torn away'.

For some years after attempts began to measure the heights of
Scottish hills, other contenders such as Ben Macdhui, were
thought by some to be the highest and though toward the end of
the 18th century the Reverend George Skene Keith decided, on
the basis of his own and his son's surveys, in favour of Ben Nevis

it was not until 1847 that Ordnance Survey measurements on Ben Macdhui finally deposed the latter. Early travellers began making the ascent in the 18th century and in 1818 Keats compared it to the 'task of mounting ten St. Pauls without the convenience of a staircase'; but it was only in 1880 that the citizens of Fort William accorded to Wm. W. Naismith and two friends the accolade of 'first ascent without guides'. From about this date the ascent began to gather popular interest and once the pony track from Achintee to the summit had been constructed in 1883 for the servicing of the Observatory, each summer saw a regular stream of tourists. Ten years later the first proposal was made for a railway to the summit, and various schemes were floated during the following twenty years. Published plans were for $4\frac{3}{4}$ miles of rack railway with a maximum gradient of 1 in 2.62 on the slopes above the Red Burn.

The establishment of the Observatory and its 20 years life make a fascinating story most engagingly told by Wm. T. Kilgour in his book *Twenty Years on Ben Nevis* (1905). To a large extent the Observatory was the child of Clement L. Wragge (depicted in newspapers of the day as the 'inclement rag') who with the support of the Scottish Meteorological Society, spent two years in compiling meteorological data with the aim of demonstrating the value of a summit observatory. From 1st June until 1st November, in both 1881 and 1882, he made a daily ascent to the summit starting at 4.00 a.m. and recording en route data at several stations. (He used the old track from Lochy Bridge—the site of the Distillery—that followed above the woods the eastern side of Allt Coire an Lochain to the Lochan Meall an t-Suidhe and though this path is shown on the 1877 First Edition of the Ordnance Survey One Inch to One Mile as continuing to the summit, it must have been rough going above the lochan). His dedication was soon rewarded and the Observatory was opened in October 1883.

Wm. T. Kilgour's book was published with the intention of raising public support for the reopening of the Observatory and is far from being a dry, scientific record. (Determined enquirers should find a copy in the larger reference libraries.) Statistics, however, it did contain and they have a fascination of their own—240 inches of rainfall in 1898 (extrapolated to give a figure of 240,000 tons of water falling on the summit area); mean annual temperature 31.4°F (for the same 11 year period 47.4°F at Fort William); worst gales, between 80 and 150 m.p.h., recorded from the south-east quadrant; lightning struck the Observatory on several occasions (in June 1895 fusing the telegraph apparatus—now in the possession of the Scottish Meteorological Society—and setting the wainscotting on fire). Even more interesting, though, is the insight given by the chapter entitled 'Some entries from the log' and a random sample indicates something of the personal regret felt by Kilgour at the closure of the Observatory.

1884 Jan. 6th —Everything covered with ice, either solid or crystalline. At 4 h. thermometer box was frozen so fast that it needed a chisel to open it. At 10 h., some snow-flakes about 1-inch diameter were observed.

Feb 16th —Owing to storm, every observation taken by two observers roped together. At 20 h. as soon as Mr. Omond went outside door of snow porch, he was lifted off his feet and blown back against Mr. Rankin, who was knocked over.

Mar. 1st —Snow porch at outer door is now about 33 ft long, with a rise of about 12 feet in its floor.

1886 Apr. 21st —Meteor as bright as first mag. star seen at 23 h. 5 m. It went from Pole Star towards W.N.W. horizon, and left a train about 10° long at a height of about 50°, which remained visible for a second.

1887 Oct. 29th —At 1 h. 5 m. St. Elmo's Fire was seen in jets 3 to 4 inches long on every point on the top of the tower, and on the top of the kitchen chimney. Owing to the number of jets on each cup of the anemometer, this instrument was quite ablaze. On the kitchen chimney, the jets on the top of the cowl were vertical, and those on the lower edge of same horizontal. While standing on office roof watching the display, the observer felt an electric sensation at his temples, and the second assistant observed that his companion's hair was glowing. At 1 h. 15 m. the accompanying hissing noise ceased, and the fire vanished from every point the same instant.

1888 Sep. 19th — Very fine sunrise. Just before the sun rose, long pink streamers were seen diverging from E. horizon, passing over-head, and converging to W., where a rosy belt topped the earth shadow.

1890 Feb. 20th — The crystals on the anemometer were today fully 7 feet long.

1891 Apr. 13th — Beautiful snow crystals falling in the afternoon; not in any measurable quantity, only a few now and again; are perfect hexagons, some in star and others in glassy disc shape. Most had small motes of dry snow attached to them, and these motes were always on one side only.

1892 Sep. 21st — A Magnificent aurora seen from 20 h. till midnight. There were three distinct arches from W. and S. to N.E., with shifting streamers shooting to the zenith.

Though the descent of Tower Ridge on 3rd September 1892 is generally considered to be the first mountaineering venture on the Ben, Wm. W. Naismith reported (SMCJ, I, p. 221) a discussion in 1889 with the Observatory staff of a climbable gully in the northern precipices, and, mountaineering ability among the staff is evidenced by a report in Kilgour's book that 'Mr. Rankin and two others descended the Tower Ridge, crossing "The Gap", with a couple of cameras'.

Snow can, and does, fall on any day of the year on the Ben and rarely in recent years has the snowfield at the foot of Observatory Gully completely disappeared. However whilst 1933 was reported to be the first year for a century in which such a snowfield did not last through the summer (the Observatory staff during the years 1883–1904 had considered it and other drifts to be permanent and, even earlier, observers such as Bishop Pocock (1760), Wilkinson (1787) and Thomas Pennant (1796) spoke of snow lasting throughout the year) Professor

Gordon Manley's careful survey (SMCJ, XXX, p. 4) takes the cautious view that the mean temperature would need to drop by 2°C for 15 years to produce a budding glacier. He goes on to show the unlikelihood of such a sequence and concludes that late snowfall in March and April are the cause of snowfields lasting through the summer.

Like the group of superb cliffs in Glencoe, Ben Nevis owes its tough andesite to the ancient foundering of a great mass of schist overlaid with thick layers of lava, which were subsequently protected from erosion and now stand proud above the Allt a Mhuillin. This durable rock covers an area of c. 1 mile in diameter and extends from Carn Dearg North-west to include the summit area and the great cirque of cliffs above the Allt a Mhuillin: it is encircled by a sea of granite that reaches down into Glen Nevis and produces the pink boulders that litter Carn Mor Dearg. Though not as rough in texture as the rhyolite of Buachaille Etive Mór, the rock on the northern cliffs is ideal for climbing, weathering to produce positive features and, on the easier routes such as the main ridges, a good supply of incut holds. Away from the ridges, however, route-finding problems are of a high order and particularly on the great, north-west face of North-east Buttress—named the Orion Face by J. H. B. Bell— the easiest line is rarely obvious.

Two excellent guide-books detail the rock-climbing and the winter routes on Ben Nevis. J. R. Marshall's *Ben Nevis* (1979 ed. with Supplement) is a comprehensive guide, very accurate in its location of routes and with very clear diagrams: it is complemented by A. C. Stead's *Rock and Ice Climbs in Lochaber and Badenoch*, a selective guide which contains 12 photographs illustrating rock and winter routes. Both include detail of the low-lying crags above Polldubh, which, facing south, are often dry and warm when conditions are poor on the higher crags. With the existence of two such guides, only those easier routes that are obvious topographical features will be described.

There is no need to make the claim that one's granny could walk up the pony track—she can be seen complete in high-heeled sandals on a clear, summer's day. Before her have trundled wheel-barrows, motor-cycles, a car and even a piano. Recent improvements to the track from Achintee and, to that joining it from the Youth Hostel, have made the ascent to the

Lochan Meall an t'Suidhe an easy walk indeed, but beyond, the crossing of the Red Burn and the zig-zags above are not suited to sandals. In winter descent the area above the Red Burn deserves a cautious approach as the ground drops away steeply to the left and, unless visibility is good, the crossing point of the deep channel made by the Red Burn, is not obvious. Again caution is needed when crossing the summit area in winter, for where the summer path flattens out near the top it veers away from the deep indentation made by Gardyloo Gully and in winter there is a tendency to cut across this angle—such a line carries perilously close to the gully whose cornice has been measured as extending 5.2 m horizontally.

For those seeking a walking route away from the summer crowds on the pony track, the steep slopes immediately above the car-park at the Glen Nevis road end, though lessening little in angle, lead to a fine ridge that gives views west into the enormous bowl of Coire Eòghainn and east to the long ridge of Aonach Mor, while higher, once it runs into the slopes above the Carn Mor Dearg Arête, the splendid complexity of the Little Brenva Face (i.e. the south-east face of North-east Buttress) can be studied. Close under the summit near to the head of this ridge at 167712, there is a spring that very rarely runs dry.

On a clear day, preferably in winter or under a north-westerly airstream, there is undoubtedly an extensive view from the summit and not even the eye of faith is needed to pick out the Cuillins, the Paps of Jura, or even the Ochils in the south-east. However, such a view is as nothing compared to the splendour of the great cirque of crags above the Allt a' Mhuillin and the three hours taken to reach the head of the glen is amply repaid as one wanders ant-like under the glacier-smoothed apron beneath Coire na Ciste, turreted high on the skyline with the Comb and Trident Buttresses.

There are three walking routes into the glen of the Allt a' Mhuillin. The easiest going will be found on the track from Achintee to the Lochan Meall an t'Suidhe past which to the east, faint and boggy paths lead north across the open bealach to a sudden drop. From this point a more easily identified path makes a descending traverse across the steep slopes beneath Carn Dearg's north face. Both other paths converge at a dam across the Allt a'Mhuillin, the first starting at the southern edge of the Distillery and the second 1 km north where a path leads under the railway from the golf club house. Neither path allows access dry-shod with the crucial section occurring a little above the old tramway—the northerly option sports a particularly well developed bog at this point that has swallowed boulders, old railway sleepers and other aids that have been carried up in attempts to avoid knee-deep plunges. While the pony-track from Achintee involves the greatest distance, in anything but a drought it is certainly the most comfortable approach.

From the paths beside the Allt a' Mhuillin there is a satisfying complexity to the crags above and many features cannot be seen from this depth. All four main ridges are, however, easily identified in clear weather. *Castle Ridge*, the first, is directly above the point where the Allt a' Mhuillin splits in two for a short distance (165725) and, if the first 100 m are avoided to the left by scrambling up the bed of North Castle Gully, need involve no more than Moderate scrambling. Once past the C.I.C. Hut (the property of the Scottish Mountaineering Club) bouldery slopes rise steeply to the foot of the Douglas Boulder, which forms a shapely cone at the foot of Tower Ridge and is noteworthy as a viewpoint. It can be circumvented by easy scrambling up either its East or West Gully but both are unpleasantly loose and the obvious ridge overlooking West Gully— *South-west Ridge* 170 m Moderate—makes a better route. *Tower Ridge* itself is a mountaineering route of great length where difficulties and variety increase with height but where no pitch is harder than Difficult. Views both near and far become more spectacular as one progresses and those on their first visit will see ahead at the Tower Gap a degree of exposure that belies the Difficult grading.

In winter Tower Ridge is a magnificent expedition fully deserving its Grade III designation: it can be very time-consuming and knowledge of the ground from a previous, summer ascent is a great advantage. There are three points worthy of mention: starting from Observatory Gully on the craggy slopes to the left of East Gully is usually the quickest approach particularly if icy conditions prevail; in most conditions the easiest climbing will be found to the left of the crest even when there is a steep ice-fall left of the Little Tower; an escape into Observatory Gully can be made by continuing on the level of the Eastern Traverse at the

Great Tower, but those then descending, perhaps in darkness, should traverse directly across to the eastern side of the gully to avoid a fall line above the steep ice of 'Tower Scoop'.

When the Douglas Boulder has been skirted *Observatory Ridge* comes into view as a buttress protruding out into Observatory Gully and soaring up to taper and flatten into the face. Zero Gully is seen as a deep recess to the left of the ridge and the vast wall to the left again—the Orion Face—imparts a sense of enormous scale. Although they have the same summer grading of Difficult, the technical standard of some pitches on Observatory Ridge is a little harder than those found on Tower Ridge. Also route finding is more of a factor on the former and if the easiest line is not found, pitches of Very Difficult must be climbed. Both ridges have their share of debris on ledges and with its higher angle, falling stones, usually moved by human agency, have caused accidents on Observatory Ridge. This route is almost as fine an outing as Tower Ridge and though shorter by 200 m, most parties new to the area seem to take longer on it.

The stark and challenging outline of *North-east Buttress* is unmistakable from the upper reaches of the Allt a'Mhuillin, as is its First Platform but the most obvious and direct route to the ridge from Observatory Gully—*Slingsby's Chimney* Moderate 125 m—has a surprisingly awkward and usually wet pitch at mid-height and *Raeburns 18 Minute Route* (Moderate 140 m) following the wall north of Slingsby's Chimney is pleasanter. Above the First Platform sound, steep rock at Very Difficult standard can be followed by keeping to the right of the broad crest: most of the ground to the left offers easier and more broken climbing. At the Second Platform the ridge narrows and leads via a steep wall to the Mantrap—this short, bulging nose is always awkward and doubly so when wet: it has defeated parties in winter. There is an avoiding movement but as this takes a line to the right of great exposure and involves crossing slabs at Difficult standard, its escape value it dubious and those setting out to climb the North-east Buttress should consider it as the hardest of the four classic ridges on Ben Nevis.

A good introduction to winter mountaineering and one quickly reached for a day's outing from the car-park beyond Polldubh, will be found in *Bob-run*. Lying in the corner where the Brenva Face turns to meet the Carn Mor Dearg Arête and, starting at a height of over 1000 m, it is a natural ice-trap and holds climbing conditions from December to April: it is often bulging with ice when other straightforward routes such as the Castle Gullies show only sad remnants and it is less prone to avalanche than the easy gullies, though care should be taken in spring when early-morning sunshine floods the top of the Brenva Face and causes stone-fall onto the longer routes of Cresta and Slalom. In approach from the south the rim of Coire Leis should be left a little way above the abseil posts and a descending traverse made over steep snow. There are usually two ice-pitches, one of the foot and another above mid-height and, though not a serious route, it can feel extravagant for a Grade II.

Winter descent to the Allt a' Mhuillin is problematical and a careful study of the topography before a first visit is well worthwhile. The shortest descent and the easiest gully is *Number Four* which lies almost 1 km north-west and c. 170 m below the summit cairn. This bland statement hides—as usually does the cloud—the 45° arc that has to be traversed and the confusing terrain where the descent flattens out at *Number 3 Gully*; however the latter's uppermost slopes are split by a distinctive and flat-headed sheaf of rock and a little beyond *Number 4* should be identifiable by a metal marker post (only very occasionally is this covered by snow). Often a short abseil over an overhanging cornice, is worthwhile from this post.

Another descent used as much for continuing along the Carn Mor Dearg Arête as for descending to the Allt a'Mhuillin also demands careful navigation for it carries close to the convex slope above the headwall of Coire Leis—with its south-eastern exposure the deep snow cover on this slope can convert to ice. To reach the Arête a bearing of 130° (true) should be followed for 400 yd from the orange-painted mountain-rescue shelter; then turn due east and further descent soon leads to the flattening at c. 1200 m level where the line of abseil posts runs down into Coire Leis. Some posts are no longer secure and their repair has not yet been decided upon, however in very icy conditions inexperienced parties might be glad of them. Certainly all other options for descent into Coire Leis from the Arête are steeper. Obviously some degree of winter mountaineering experience is necessary for these two descents to be

127

accomplished with comfort and safety. But it is just as important for those descending by the pony-track to have a map and compass and the ability to use them in adverse conditions—in the last decade several parties have veered south from the path and have come to grief on the steep slopes, split by deep gullies, of Coire Eòghainn: further on, the easy-angled ridge leading down to Carn Dearg South-west bemuses those perhaps only a little off course but again there is no easy winter descent from this top.

*Carn Mór Dearg (1223 m), Carn Dearg Meadhonach (1180 m)

From the Mamores to the south or when approaching from the north by way of the Allt Daim, the winter view of Carn Mór Dearg is positively Alpine. It forms an elongated, south-north ridge with moderate slopes falling to the Allt a'Mhuillin but much steeper slopes interrupted by three fine ridges to the east. The southern tail of the hill's spine curls round to form the Carn Mor Dearg Arête, by which it is joined to Ben Nevis. With its great height—1058 m at its lowest—and with its genuinely sharp crest, the Arête often forms a tight-rope of névé and is, in such conditions, an exhilarating outing. Both sides of the Arête fall away very steeply indeed and though no definite lines present themselves, there is winter mountaineering among the crags above Coire Leis and also on the east face. To traverse from Carn Mór Dearg to Ben Nevis on a clear winter's day is an outing unique in the British Isles, for the vast spread of crag between North-east Buttress and Carn Dearg Buttress is perfectly complimented by the slender elegance of the Arête.

The length of the summit ridge is composed of a pink granite and lies within the ring of granite surrounding Ben Nevis core of ancient lava. Bouldery slopes cover the crest and make the Arête itself in summer—so aptly described by Geikie as 'a mass of ruin, like the shattered foundations of an ancient rampart'—a place for nimble feet.

Most ascents of Carn Mór Dearg are made by way of the Allt a'Mhuillin; however the hill can be reached from Glen Nevis following the course of the Allt Coire Giubhsachan and starting at Old Steall. This approach leads to the foot of the east ridge which is well defined and often in winter forms its own arête.

There are two other easterly ridges and that leading directly to the summit of Carn Dearg Meadhonach, with a pinnacle near the top, makes a fine winter route.

At various points from the ridge between the two main tops a very long glissade of up to 500 m can be made down to the Allt a'Mhuillin. Frequently in spring the right conditions occur for this exhilarating plunge and, if a lucky course leads into one of the drainage channels, the downward swoop can be as brief as nerve allows.

Accommodation

Apart from the accommodation mentioned in chapter 8 (see p. 116) at Fort William, SYHA, Steall Cottage and camp-sites in Glen Nevis, there is the CIC Hut by the Allt a'Mhuillin. This latter is under heavy demand and prior, and early booking through an affiliated club is needed. A few dry, sheltered sites for camping will be found beside the Allt a'Mhuillin, roughly 1 km above the dam. The orange summit shelter and two others at 173714 (Coire Leis) and 158719 (Carn Dearg North-west) are intended as emergency bivouacs with maximum capacity of eight seated adults. Removal of the two latter shelters is under debate. That in Coire Leis is difficult to find in its boulder field and can be entirely covered by snow in heavy winters.

References

Twenty Years on Ben Nevis, Wm. T. Kilgour (O.P.).

Climber's Guide to Ben Nevis, G. G. MacPhee (SMC 1936—now out of print). This edition contained the complete summit panorama in four folding sections, originally drawn by James E. Shearer in 1895.

Climber's Guide to Ben Nevis, J. R. Marshall (SMC 1979).

Mountaineering in Scotland, W. H. Murray. Diadem Compendium edition, 1982.

A Progress in Mountaineering, J. H. B. Bell (O.P.).

The SMC Journal in the last 93 years has hundreds of notes, references, and articles about Ben Nevis. The following is a personal selection.

Vol. III, p. 323. Hospitality in the Observatory after the second ascent of North-east Buttress. Wm. Brown.

Vol. V, p. 45. Hospitality at 8.30pm. New Year 1898 in the Observatory. '16 hours on the Ben', W. I. Clark.

Vol. V, p. 87. Note on a winter climb on the west face of the Carn Mor Dearg Arête.

Vol. VI, p. 213. The Observatory Ridge, H. Raeburn. First ascent (solo) 1901.

Vol. VII, p. 195. From Sea to Summit, H. Raeburn. A fine article that mentions in passing the first, solo ascent of Observatory Buttress.

Vol. IX, p. 153. A Scottish Ice Climb, H. Raeburn. The first ascent in 1906 of Green Gully.

Vol. XXI, p. 200. Zero Gully, J. H. B. Bell. Article describing an ascent combining Slav Route and Zero Gully, and an indication of what winter climbing standards were in 1936.

Vol. XXII, p. 367. A Ben Nevis Constellation of Climbs, J. H. B. Bell. A summary of the author's outstanding exploration of the Orion Face.

Vol. XXVII, p. 107. Modern Scottish Winter Climbing, J. R. Marshall. A definitive summary at the time—1962.

Vol. XXX, p. 4. Scotland's Permanent Snows, G. Manley.

63. *The Tower Gap.*   *Peter Hodgkiss*

64. *Centurion: 1st Pitch.* *Peter Hodgkiss*

65.   *Descending from the Ben toward the Carn Mor Dearg Arête.*   *W. Mockridge*

66.   *The north face of Ben Nevis. Tower Ridge starts bottom right and North-east Buttress b*

entre.

Peter Hodgkiss

67.   *Carn Dearg Meadhonach from the north. Aonach Beag to the left.*   *Peter Hodgkiss*

68. *Looking down on Steall Flats.*   *Richard Gibbens*

69.   *Aonach Beag from the lip of Coire Giubhsachan.*   *Richard Gibbens*

69a.   Stob Bàn from Cruach Innse. The giant's staircase of quartzite slabs dropping from the bealach is thought to have been scoured by a glacial tongue flowing west, i.e. uphill.

Peter Hodgkiss

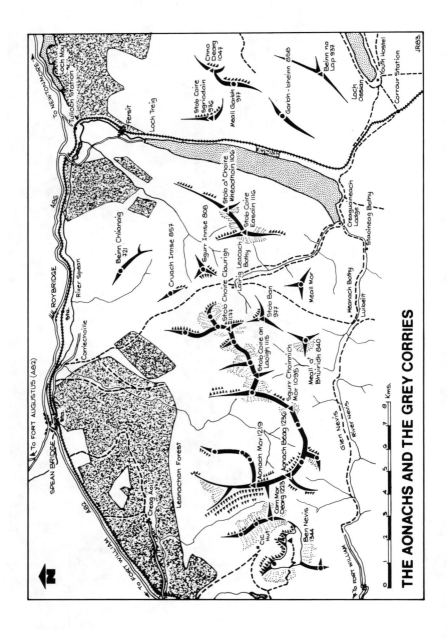

THE AONACHS AND THE GREY CORRIES

10

The Aonachs
and the Grey Corries

*Aonach Mór (1219 m)
  Stob an Cul Choire (1097 m)
*Aonach Beag (1236 m)
  Stob Coire Bhealaich (1097 m)
  Sgurr a' Bhuic (965 m)
  Sgurr Choinnich Beag (966 m)
*Sgurr Choinnich Mor (1095 m)
  Stob Coire Easain (1080 m)
  Beinn na Socaich (1007 m)
*Stob Coire an Laoigh (1115 m)
  Stob Coire Cath na Sine (1080 m)
  Stob Coire Leith (1105 m)
*Stob Choire Claurigh (1177 m)
  Stob Coire na Ceannain (1121 m)
  Stob Coire Gaibhre (930 m)
*Stob Ban (977 m)
  Cruach Innse (857 m)
  Sgurr Innse (808 m)
*Stob Coire Easain (1116 m)
*Stob a' Choire Mheadhoin (1106 m)

Lying between Glen Nevis and Glen Spean, these hills form to
Ben Nevis an elongated tail stretching eastwards, with one deep
gap at the Lairig Leacach, to the boundary formed by Loch
Treig. Most of the Grey Corries are built of the same quartzite
that gives such distinctive whiteness to the bare summits of the
Mamores, and thus the name Grey Corries, but the northerly
spurs do not form quite such sharp arêtes. The great forest of
Leanachan to the north restricts access in this arc, but an
excellent track through the Larig Leacach is compensation to the
north-east, and the forest can be penetrated from the north-west

at Torlundy. Still on the northern fringes there are two fine rivers, the Cour and the Spean—both worthy of visits in their own right. While the first can be followed in descent from the hills (and is described later), the Spean deserves a half-day, preferably in spring or autumn for appreciation of the deciduous woodland along its southern shore. A little-used, and single-track driving road runs from Spean Bridge to Coire-choille, where the tarmac ends and a footpath continues beyond Insh. Footbridges cross the river $1\frac{1}{2}$ km east of Roy Bridge and also at the Glenspean Lodge Hotel: between these two bridges and further east there are a series of waterfalls on a grand scale.

Access to these hills from Glen Nevis involves, with the exception of Aonach Beag, both great distance and rough ground, though a camp near the watershed or use of Steall Cottage, makes the traverse of all the tops between the Lairig Leacach and Aonach Beag feasible. For those planning use of the West Highland Line—and the station at Roy Bridge is convenient for approach to the Lairig Leacach—there is a useful adjunct in the summer bus service (July and August only) plying between Fort William and Glen Nevis (Phone 0397-2373 for details).

The Aonachs
Aonach Mór (1219 m), **Stob an Cul Choire** (1097 m),
Aonach Beag (1236 m), **Stob Coire Bhealaich** (1097 m),
Sgurr a' Bhuich (965 m)

Somewhat overshadowed in its proximity to Ben Nevis and not easy of access, this range has a pleasant air of seclusion accentuated for those who wander into the vast, eastern corries. In spring the series of eastern corries beneath Aonach Beag and Aonach Mor's southern shoulder are a wonderland where great snow-beds push snouts into the corrie-beds and form moraines, where burns spout over ice-falls in the ravines that have been scored deeply into the lower cliffs and where ranks of *roches moutonnées* point their striae north-east. On the head-walls masses of rock occur apparently haphazardly, sometimes as isolated buttresses beneath the cornice rim and, less often as ridges reaching up to breach it, but all of mountaineering interest and mainly composed of compact, rough schist.

Aonach Mór (1219 m)

Of greater bulk than its taller neighbour, and thus its Gaelic name given before the advent of the Ordnance Survey, it offers easy-angled slopes to the north reached by way of the public road from Torlundy (7 km north-east of Fort William) to Creag Aoil, where passing places just short of the working quarry have been enlarged and permit parking. A little east of the quarry at a gate across the road a right turn carries south into the forest and should be followed, ignoring a second right turn, to a clearing where traces of the old tramway can be found. The track continues beyond the south-western corner of the clearing, above which the course of the Allt an t-Sneachda and open hillside is soon reached.

If descending into Leanachan Forest late in the day, either from Aonach Mor or further east from the Grey Corries, it is well to have a clear idea of the route to be followed. There are a multiplicity of tracks confusingly alike, not all of which are shown on the O.S. 1:50,000 map.

With the gathering ground of the extensive summit plateau the eastern corries of Aonach Mór hold snow throughout most years—it is claimed that Roy Bridge Railway Station is the only one in Britain from which snow can be seen all year round. Great quantities of snow also last into most summers in the open corrie to the north, containing the Allt an t-Sneachda— burn of the snow, although local people know it as Coire nan Geadh (corrie of the goose) from the shape of the snow remnants that forms in most summers. An excellent ski-run, often of 2 km with 600 m of descent, can be enjoyed away from the crowds in this corrie, although outline planning permission has already been granted to a development company for the construction of an access road and ski tows. Fickle, Atlantic weather may yet preserve the solitude of this corrie.

Despite its great area the summit plateau of Aonach Mór is a ridge clearly defined by very steep slopes falling on both sides and throughout its 2 km length. In thick weather and particularly under snow its featureless character is confusing and finding both the bealach for continuation south onto Aonach Beag and, the only safe winter descent—from 193724 west to the bealach under Carn Mor Dearg—needs careful compass work.

In winter both flanks are of mountaineering interest, the western face being a complex of ill-defined buttresses and gullies at their steepest under the actual summit, while to the east two open corries with steep headwalls offer snow climbs. Sporting routes will also be found on the three ridges that define the corrie boundaries while the most northerly corrie—Coire an Lochain—is interrupted by short, steep ribs of granite. The southern-most, bounding ridge—found almost due east from the summit cairn and leading down to the bealach beneath Stob an Cul Choire—whilst only a summer scramble is often badly iced in winter and requires confidence in the use of axe and crampons for those descending unroped. South of this ridge lies the recess of the aptly named An Cul Choire—the rearmost corrie—and near the centre of its headwall a fine ridge rears up above a broad apron of equally steep rock. By its easiest line the ridge has a standard of Difficult and gives roughly 140 m of climbing before levelling off into a short arete beneath easy scrambling to Aonach Mór's southern slopes near a point on the O.S. 1:25,000 map given the name 'Seang Aonach Mor'—thus *Aonach Seang* (slender ridge) would seem an appropriate name for so fine a feature. In summer it can be reached most conveniently by a descent over steep scree from the bealach between Aonach Mór and Aonach Beag, but in winter (when the ridge offers a worthwhile climb at Grade III) these slopes are avalanche prone and often guarded by large cornices.

Stob an Cul Choire (1097 m), Tom na Sroine (981 m)

When climbing Aonach Mor from the north, return over these tops which are in effect a north-eastern arm of the larger hill, makes a pleasant circuit, though in icy conditions descent of Aonach Mor's east ridge demands some mountaineering technique if not a rope. The bealach at the foot of this ridge is a spectacular place: facing south the ground drops away steeply into An Cul Choire above which towers the outline of Aonach Beag's North-east Ridge while closer at hand a steep slope sweeps up to the right and a narrow, rocky ridge is immediately above on the left.

The ridge between Stob an Cul Choire and Tom na Sroine is narrow and the steeper ground beneath the crest to the south and east develops into crags which as the ridge turns north become very steep indeed. From the bump on the ridge known as Stob Coire an Fhir Dhuibh a wall of schist stretches for perhaps 1 km but rarely attains more height than 100 m.

Descending north from Tom na Sroine there is a small dam across the Allt Choille-rais at the forest edge. Not 100 yds lower a new land rover track winds down through the afforestation to the line of the old tramway.

Aonach Beag (1236 m)

Joined to its neighbour Aonach Mór at a high bealach of c. 950 m, Aonach Beag has nevertheless a different and more complex form. It differs also in being composed mainly of ancient schists whereas Aonach Mór falls within the great circle of granite surrounding Ben Nevis. A straightforward ascent can be made from Old Steall (in ruins) where a bridge crosses the Allt Coire Guibhsachan. Above open slopes lead north to the toe of the south-west ridge. More repaying is the traverse of the series of tops north-east of Old Steall, starting with the sharp cone of Sgurr a'Bhuic so prominent in views from the east, and continuing over the twin tops of Stob Coire Bhealaich. Parts of this ridge are steep enough to require care when icy conditions prevail and, its upper part including the summit plateau builds out enormous cornices above the north-eastern face.

The mountaineering potential on Aonach Beag was recognised almost a century ago by Norman Collie who recommended its *North-east Ridge* to William Naismith. Naismith very properly made the first ascent in winter (April 1895) with Maclay and Thomson, for it is under these conditions that the ridge becomes a fine expedition (Grade II/III: 460 m). Not least of its attractions is its remoteness and the approach from upper Glen Nevis of over three hours makes the sight of another party a rare occurrence. In its later stages this approach has confused and even confounded many parties for, in poor visibility, picking a good line across the corrie to find the foot of the ridge is no easy matter. From Old Steall it is quicker to follow the line of the path east for 2 km before striking north to the bealach just west of Sgurr Choinnich Beag—traversing the southern slopes of Sgurr a'Bhuic over ground seamed by deep drainage channels is exasperatingly slow. If a clear view can be had from the bealach a terrace will be discerned traversing the corrie at the 700 m

137

level, i.e 30 m beneath the level of the bealach; but the ridge itself is not properly seen from this point. In thick weather a better policy is to descend 100 m from the bealach and then in a line north-north-west, cross three burns the second and third of which are ravine-like: at the fourth burn the North-east Ridge is immediately above. The apparent map distance of 2 km across the corrie is no measure and unless conditions are good both underfoot and overhead, a minimum time of one hour should be expected.

The scale of this north-eastern face can only properly be studied and appreciated from the head of the tortuous glen issuing the burn with three names, first Allt a'Chuil Choire, then lower Allt Coire an Eoin, and lastly the Cour (a similar but more distant viewpoint is Stob Coire Easain). From this angle the aptness of the Gaelic name, An Aghaidh Gharbh (the rough face) is very clear, as is the climbing potential. The following routes waited 80 years before Collie's recommendation was taken up once more.

The Ramp   300 m   Grade III

Approaching from Glen Nevis, this climb is found about a mile before the North East Ridge of Aonach Beag, with which it can easily be confused on a clear day by experienced parties. (G. R. NN 206712). Just north of the Aonach Beag-Sgurr Choinnich Beag col, a prominent buttress falls into the corrie on the east flank of Stob Coire Bhealaich. This is the (unnamed) top, half a mile south east of Aonach Beag. The buttress is attached to the top by an obvious ridge. Left of the crest of the buttress is a long, tapering snow slope which appears from below to be a couloir. It is, in fact, a ramp rising through a fairly steep face, and in the good snow conditions encountered gave an excellent, long climb.

Climb the ramp, several pitches, to the top (240 m). Continue by the ridge to the summit, very exposed on the left (60 m).
K. V. Crocket, R. Hockey, B. E. H. Maden and R. Pillinger,
February 1975.

Anabasis   240 m   Grade III

High on the East Face, facing the Grey Corries, is a steep buttress, from which a band of more broken rocks slant up rightwards to just below the summit. The buttress rises above a basin reached by a long and complicated approach up steep slopes broken by deep gullies and rocky outcrops. The climb starts up a steep snow-ice gully at the lowest point of the buttress. A bergschrund was crossed on the first ascent.

Steepening snow gains the gully which leads in three pitches (rock belays on right) to a deep cave where the gully ends beneath overhangs (60 m). Traverse right on to ice bulge and climb to rightward trending snow shelf below upper rocks (23 m). Continue rising traverse until an open groove can be climbed into a shallow bay (30 m). A short ice groove on the left leads to mixed ground, trending right via rock ridge to reach the upper snow slope (37 m). Follow right edge to nose which breaks through massive cornices close to the summit (90 m).
R. A. Croft and J. R. Sutcliffe, April 1973.

Approach to the next route described could be quicker via the bealach between Aonach Beag and Aonach Mor, but in certain winter conditions this descent would be dangerous.

Mayfly   210 m   Grade III
There is a large triangular face between the Aonach Mór—Aonach Beag saddle and the North-East Ridge of Aonach Beag. The face has a steep buttress nearest the col, a gully area in the centre, and the lower, rocky part of the Ridge. Just left of the centre (GR 197 718), an initially wide gully, marked on its lower right by a rock rib, leads to above the pinnacles of the North-East Ridge. This climb takes the gully.

Climb the gully 90 m to reach an 18 m high and equally wide icefall. This is climbed on its right to continue by the much narrower gully above, which leads via a steep ice pitch with an awkward bulge to the easier but icy top section. Finish along the North-East Ridge to the summit.
K. Schwartz, May 1979.

High on the west face of Aonach Beag a line of crags provides more climbing. From the road end in Glen Nevis they can be seen in line of sight between Meall Cumhann and the lower slopes of Ben Nevis: they are also an obvious feature when ascending the glen of the Allt Giubhsachan above Old Steall. From this angle the outline of a very steep crag can be seen (Skyline Buttress—no recorded ascent) and the following routes commence 100 yd north of this buttress in a bay containing a prominent chimney. The rock is a hard, brittle schist.

Crevassed Rib   100 m   Difficult
Climb the buttress right of the chimney turning the steep, upper slab on the inside of the gully. (This steep, upper slab was included by J. Smith and G. S. Johnstone in a later ascent, making the route Very Difficult).
Mr. and Mrs. G. S. Johnstone, September 1951.

North Buttress   100 m   Difficult
The buttress left of the chimney though steep is not as formidable as appearance suggests.
M. Coventry and W. V. Thomas, September 1951.

North of the bay containing these two routes is a greater expanse of rock, the western crest of which is taken by the following route.

Raw Egg Buttress   170 m   Very Difficult
Start in a short chimney beneath a prominent cave. Above traverse left to reach the edge, then follow easiest line and finish by a steep chimney.
J. A. Brown, B. H. Humble and T. D. MacKinnon, May 1938.

There is a considerable area of rock south of these routes and no winter ascents have been recorded hereabouts.

Grey Corries

Stob Coire Gaibhre (930 m), ***Stob Choire Claurigh** (1177 m),
Stob Coire na Ceannain (1121 m), **Stob a' Choire Leith** (1105 m),
Stob Coire Cath na Sine (1080 m), **Caisteal** (1104 m),
***Stob Coire an Laoigh** (1115 m), **Stob Coire Easain** (1080 m),
***Sgurr Choinnich Mór** (1095 m), **Sgurr Choinnich Beag** (966 m),
***Stob Bàn** (997 m)

This great roll-call of peaks complete with four Munros, flatters to deceive for the ridge running c. 8 km from north-east to south-west maintains its height falling beneath 914 m only at its last bealach—that between Sgurr Choinnich Mor and Beag—and all the tops can be traversed in the course of a summer's day. Unless, however, one has a camp near the Glen Nevis watershed this fine hill-walk is probably best enjoyed when travelling through the hills for the distance involved in a round trip from either Coire-choille or from Glen Nevis is over 30 km.

From Coire-choille, reached either from Roy Bridge Station and the bridge over the Spean 1.5 km east, or by the single-track road from beside the Spean Bridge Hotel (so fine is the river scenery, the Scots pine and the broad-leaf woodland along this stretch of road that it seems a pity to drive it), the old drove road runs up the eastern margin of the Leanachan Forest and through the Lairig Leacach. (This ancient track is a right-of-way.) There is a locked gate just north of the old tramway but the track beyond is negotiable only for four-wheel drive vehicles. At the northern limit of the forest easy slopes lead up to Beinn Bhàn and over the minor top of **Stob Coire Gaibhre** to **Stob Choire Claurigh**, but this approach, though pleasant enough, by-passes the finest feature at this end of the ridge which is the double-storied corrie looming above the Lairig Leacach. Particularly in winter this great amphitheatre with an almost perfectly circular lochan nestling in the upper bowl is a delightful place. On the eastern and southern headwall there will be very steep snow slopes but terrain at an easier angle leads south-east to the summit of **Stob Coire na Ceannain**, from where the quality of this winter approach continues with the narrow ridge, often an arête of snow or ice, to Stob Choire Claurigh. Beyond the main summit the ridge undulates and twists gently to the final and appropriately sharp cone of **Sgurr Choinnich Beag**. While the terrain makes for easy going, there is one point on the ridge deserving of great caution when fresh snow lies thick on the crest. Low on the north-west ridge of **Sgurr Choinnich Mor**—at 231720—there are quartzite pavements at low-angle rent by a series of crevices parallel to the direction of the ridge, wide enough to admit a human body, and deep enough to cause serious injury. When snow-free these fissures are obvious but when snow has masked them completely—as does happen—it is well to keep to the eastern side of the crest.

Fine though this long ridge is, with spectacular views of Ben

141

Nevis towering above the great wall of Aonach Mór and Beag, merely to traverse the tops is to miss some of the hidden qualities that lie to the north. And hidden they are for the distant main road behind the expanse of the Leanachan Forest allows neither close view nor obvious access. The hub from which the northern spurs and corries are reached is Coire Choimhlidh. Either the old tramway or a Forestry Commission land-rover track (starting from 1 km north of Coire-choille) leads to a dam across the Allt Choimhlidh above the forest. From here one looks up to the twin northern spurs of **Beinn na Socaich** and Sron an Lochain enclosing Coire a'Mhadaidh with its spectacular head-wall of black crags. While appearing attractively steep these crags must class as the most rotten and loose in Scotland—during a foray in 1886 by a party of botanists who penetrated the recesses of these crags, a member of the rearguard who had served in the trenches with the Naval Brigade was heard to shout 'confound it! This is worse than the cannon balls in the Crimea; unless we remove beyond the elevation of our friends we shall get killed'. His companion on the day went on to report 'As we were speaking, a large piece of rock came past me down a perpendicular rent, which covered me with dust as it went past, filling the air with a sulphurous odour. This caused so much alarm that a retreat . . . over dangerous loose rocks, had to be accomplished at a pace which astonished my companion as well as myself . . . I am afraid some unparliamentary exclamations accidentally escaped the lips of some unclerical members . . .' The incident was rationalised and even justified . . . a mental adjustment familiar to most climbers . . . on the basis of discovering a new station for *saxifraga rivularis* and the first find for fifty years of *Saxifraga caespitosa* (true). Almost a century later the place is unchanged, though in a hard winter and on a day of deep frost, the deeply recessed gullies make fine ascents. Attractive snow climbs of an easier nature also lead from the corrie to the ridge of Beinn na Socaich.

The narrow confines of the three northern corries between Beinn na Socaich and Stob Choire Claurigh are great snow gatherers and mountain skiers can enjoy long traverses between the corries and the main ridge, which is accessible by way of hidden corridors.

On a long summer's day a most worthwhile descent to the

north is that from Sgurr Choinnich Beag down over the serried ranks of *roches moutonnées* beneath An Aghaidh Gharbh and alongside the twistings of the Cour's limestone bed. This 5 km stretch of water is a paradise of water-falls and swimming-pools of deep, green water. The water-course cuts through miniature gorges, turns through innumerable angles and from a final constriction at the corrie mouth bursts forth in a magnificent cascade. A little below this point, where there is a dam and a pipe-line, a clearing on the west bank beside the forest leads down to a bridge and the old tramway.

In an area of remote peaks, **Stob Bàn** is particularly awkward of access. Approach from the main ridge of the Grey Corries involves a descent of 300 m and a reascent over scree of the most unstable kind, while, if starting from Glen Nevis or from Corrour Railway Station the peak is perhaps best taken as one incident in a through-route. Probably the most interesting way to include it in a traverse of the Grey Corries is to cross the Lairig Leacach from the north and take to the north-east ridge beyond the bothy. From the bealach to the north of Stob Bàn there is a curious giant's staircase of quartzite that spills down east for c. 150 m: it makes an interesting descent and also a natural route to the foot of Cùl Choirean—a deeply recessed, hanging corrie and a worthy companion to Coire na Ceannain to the north (contouring from the level of the bealach into Cul Choirean involves slow going on rough and steep ground). Straightforward slopes lead from Cul Choirean onto the south-east ridge of Stob Coire na Ceannain but under Stob Choire Claurigh and the sharp ridge between the two peaks the ground is craggy and generally steep.

Stob Coire Easain (1116 m), Stob a' Choire Mheadhoin (1106 m), Sgurr Innse (808 m), Cruach Innse (857)

The two larger hills, usually known collectively as the Easains, are easily climbed from the north via the road to the dam at the foot of Loch Treig, and, return can be varied by descending the north-western corrie, Coire Easain Beag, between the two peaks and following down the course of the Allt Laire. However the convenient siting of the railway stations at Corrour and Tulloch allows a very pleasant traverse with the better views in a south-north direction when the Grey Corries, the Aonachs and Ben Nevis unfold as one progresses along the excellent path to Lochtreighead. Once beyond Creaguaineach Lodge it is worthwhile to follow the path on the north side of the Allt na Lairig for 1 km both to enjoy the gorge between Creag Ghuanach and Creagan a' Chase and to avoid the hummocky ground on the latter top. (Those with the time on a clear evening would profit from a walk up Creag Ghuanach which is perfectly placed for views of the peaks on both sides of Glen Nevis and of Buachaille Etive Mór through the narrows of Gleann na Giubhsachan).

No climbing has been recorded on these two hills though directly beneath and east of Stob a Choire Mheadhoin lies a steeply-walled coire with schist crags high on the south wall. With their north-easterly aspect, these crags may be worth a winter visit.

Despite its relatively minor stature, **Sgurr Innse** is prominent from great distances. Its barrell-like form is instantly recognisable from Buachaille Etive Mór. As the distant view suggests Sgurr and Cruach Innse are steep and rocky, but the Sgurr far outweighs its taller neighbour in this respect. Both hills can be traversed in a short day from the Lairig Leacach but for those without rock-climbing experience, the only comfortable descent of the Sgurr is down a north-westerly shelf. In fact Sgurr Innse belies its formidable appearance as its crags are too broken for much continuous climbing and only one route has been recorded on the south western aspect.

Headjam   50 m   Severe

This climb takes the obvious groove on the summit cliff facing the Lairig Leacach Bothy. Climb first 15 m up wet crack in groove and on right wall. Steeper and more difficult climbing leads to overhang split by narrow chimney-crack. Go up this to platform on left (32 m). Continue up right-trending groove and scramble to easy ground near to summit of the Sgurr (16 m).
S. J. Crymble and K. Schwartz, June 1970.

Accommodation

Details for Fort William and Glen Nevis will be found in the Mamores chapter (see p. 116).

Spean Bridge—Hotel and bed and breakfast accommodation.
Inveroy—Caravan and campsite.
Roy Bridge—Caravan and camp site (telephone 037 781 275).
Glenspean Lodge Hotel—telephone 039 781 224.

At Fersit bed and breakfast and bunkhouse accommodation are available, but there is no telephone and those coming from far afield are advised to write to Mrs. N. Smith, Fersit, by Spean Bridge, Inverness-shire. Staoineag and Meanach bothies on the Amhainn Rath, and the bothy south of the summit of the Lairig Leacach are suitable for small parties staying overnight outside the stalking season (the latter place was fitted with a telephone before the turn of the century—the accommodation is somewhat sparser now).

References

Scottish Mountains on Ski, Malcolm Slesser (West Col) (1970). For details of ski-tours in the Grey Corries.

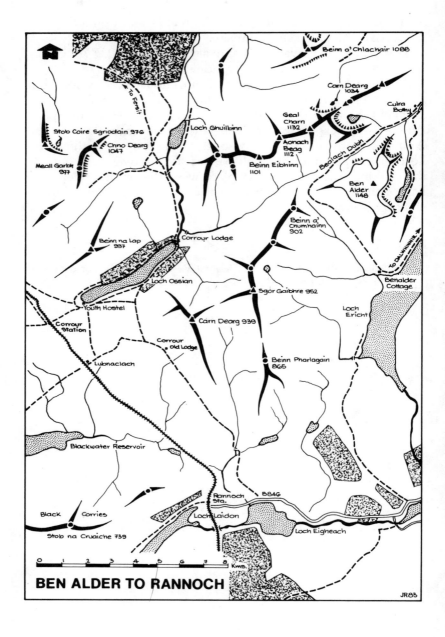

Beinn a' Chlachair 1088
Carn Dearg 1034
Culra Bothy
Geal Charn 1132
Aonach Beag 1112
Bealach Dubh
Ben Alder 1148
Stob Coire Sgriodain 976
Loch Ghuilbinn
Chno Dearg 1047
Beinn Eibhinn 1101
Meall Garbh 977
Beinn a' Chumhainn 902
Beinn na Lap 937
Corrour Lodge
Benalder Cottage
To Fersit
Loch Ossian
Sgor Gaibhre 952
Loch Ericht
Youth Hostel
Corrour Station
Carn Dearg 939
Corrour Old Lodge
To Dalwhinnie
Lubnaclach
Beinn Pharlagain 865
Blackwater Reservoir
Rannoch Sta.
B846
Black Corries
Loch Laidon
Loch Eigheach
Stob na Cruaiche 739
0 1 2 3 4 5 6 7 8 Kms.

BEN ALDER TO RANNOCH

JR83

70.	*From Meanach Bothy: Aonach Beag just left of the gable, and left again the top of North-east Buttress appears to be part of Sgurr a Bhuic.*	W. A. Bentall

71.	*Stob an Cùl Choire from Stob Coire Eàsain. The long stretch of Aonach Mór behind with the actual summit under cloud.*	Douglas Scott

72. *The dark, crumbling cliffs of Caisteil with Aonach Beag and Ben Nevis behind.*
Peter Hodgkiss

73. *Stob Coire na Ceannain from the west.*   *Peter Hodgkiss*

74. *Cruach Innse and Sgurr Innse (right) with the Lairig Leacach bothy below.*
Peter Hodgkiss

75.   *The lochan nestling in Coire na Ceannain.*   *Peter Hodgkiss*

76. On the West Highland Line approaching the snow tunnel north of Rannoch Station. The twin, snowy tops to the right are the Easains. *Peter Hodgkiss*

77. Corrour Halt: Leum Uilleam behind. *Peter Hodgkiss*

78.   *The Easains from Cruach Innse.*   *Peter Hodgkiss*

79.   *Loch Treig from the head of the loch.*   *Peter Hodgkiss*

80. *The splendid view east from Corrour Halt. The Bealach Dubh sits in the centre with Ben Alder to the right and Beinn Eibhinn to the left.* Peter Hodgkiss

81. *The old droving route now followed by the West Highland Line to Loch Treig. The shapely cone is Binnein Beag.* Peter Hodgkiss

82. *Tom Rigg—warden at Loch Ossian Youth Hostel for many summers. At other times world traveller, marathon runner, stalker, and always a raconteur.*   Peter Hodgkiss

83. *Beinn Eibhinn and Loch Ossian; 17th December 1935. (Reproduced by courtesy of The Scots Magazine—Robert M. Adam Collection.)*   Robert M. Adam

11

Ben Alder to Rannoch

*Carn Dearg (939 m)
  Beinn Pharlagain (865 m)
*Sgòr Gaibhre (952 m)
  Sgòr Choinnich (929 m)
  Meall a' Bhealaich (862 m)
  Beinn a' Chumhainn (902 m)
*Ben Alder (1148 m)
  Sron Coire na h'Iolaire (953 m)
*Beinn Bheòil (1016 m)
  The Fara (910 m)

Ben Alder to Rannoch

Despite having two railway lines adjacent to it—the West Highland Line to Rannoch and Corrour and the Inverness Line to Dalwhinnie—this area has a greater sense of remoteness than any other in the Central Highlands. For there are no public roads within the area and the only two roads near its margins— the B846 to Rannoch Station, and the A9—are at great distance from the hills. The boundaries are Loch Ericht, the West Highland Line and, to the north, a less straightforward line that follows Loch Ossian and the Uisge Labhair to cross the Bealach Dubh and then to veer north by Loch and River Pattack; thus including the wedge of land between that river and the A9. Within lies Ben Alder, fascinating in its variety of corrie and ridge and with a definite air of inaccessibility adding to its attraction. All the tops in the western half are most conveniently reached via the West Highland Line and a start from the isolated Corrour Halt adds to the refreshing aura of remoteness that attaches to these hills.

Carn Dearg, Sgòr Gaibhre, Beinn Pharlagain

A traverse of these tops from Corrour Halt to Rannoch Station,

F

i.e. between the morning and afternoon trains, makes a splendid outing. Views both far and near—of Binnein Mor and Binnean Beag's sublime outline, of the great stretch of Rannoch Moor, and of Strath Ossian's U-shaped trench—are particularly satisfying from Carn Dearg, whose slopes are at an angle easy enough to walk with hands in pocket. Indeed the whole round of these tops is characterised by the easy going which, when not under snow, is on carpets of moss and sedge, amongst which occasional clumps of moss campion blend into the muted colours. Carn Dearg's broad, western flank is traversed by a good path—'The Road to the Isles'—which commences immediately south of the Youth Hostel at Loch Ossian. This path leads eventually to Rannoch Station passing on the way the ruin of Corrour Old Lodge. As can be surmised from the substantial granite walls, the Old Lodge was a fine building, but once the railway line was installed, a new Lodge was built at the eastern end of Loch Ossian. For some time the Old Lodge was used as an isolation hospital—and no more isolated site can be imagined—but once this use ceased it lay empty until its roof was removed to avoid the pointless payment of rates.

In descent from Beinn Pharlagain the above-mentioned track can be met at the bridge over the Allt Eigheach, from which a line can be taken south-west over the moor for the railway track; but such a short cut is advisable only when dry conditions prevail underfoot for some of the bogs hereabout are truly dangerous and extremely difficult to detect even when not snow-covered. Particularly is this the case a little to the north on the moor beneath Carn Dearg's southern outpost, Sron Leachd a'Chaorruinn, where the author witnessed one unfortunate descend very quickly to his thighs—amusing enough when there was sufficient man-power for extraction but with possibly fatal consequences for the solo walker.

In winter vast herds of deer gather in the corrie between the long southern ridges—Coire Eigheach—and on its slopes beneath the Màm Ban. The very names for these hills, Corrour Forest and Rannoch Forest, are used in the sense, adopted from mediaeval times, of open ground peopled with deer.

For those walking through the hills there is an obvious continuation over **Sgòr Choinnich**, **Meall a'Bhealaich** and **Beinn a Chumhainn** with the latter providing a fine view through the Bealach Dubh to the north-east and into Coire a'Chàrra Bhig to the north.

Ben Alder (1148 m)

Like Ben Nevis, the great bulk of this hill is instantly recognisable from great distances: its steep slopes above the Bealach Dubh to the north and above the Bealach Beithe to the east distinguish it from the west and south, while from Dalwhinnie and the Drumochter Hills the snow-holding properties of its Garbh Choire is very apparent in winter. All approaches are long, though by the shortest it is possible to make the ascent inside a summer's day. This shortest route starts from Corrour Halt and follows the track along the southern shore of Loch Ossian until a bridge behind Corrour Lodge leads to a path winding north of a wood and across flats to a substantial bridge over the Uisge Labhair. What path there is beside this burn, lies on the north bank and in the usual wet conditions the 9 km to the Bealach Dubh make heavy going. Before two thirds of this distance have been covered Ben Alder's west ridge swoops down and the burn is easily crossed through the alluvial spreads that have been carried down from Coire a'Chàrra Bhig. Those following this route and planning to climb the hill in between trains will have little time to explore the vast summit plateau of almost 4.0 sq km above 1000 m or to soak in the extensive view. With its central position in the Highlands it wants only a clear day for other peaks at great distance to be picked out; for example the lowly West Lomond in Fife can be seen in the gap between Schiehallion and Carn Mairg, and the upper cone of Sgur Mòr Fannich stands out above Creag Meagaidh—at 96 and 112 km respectively.

Other approaches involve considerable distances that suppose an overnight stop in the hills. From Dalwhinnie a good track runs for 14 km beside Loch Ericht, leaving it at Ben Alder Lodge to veer west to Loch Pattack. This track is barred by locked gates but these are negotiable with a bicycle. From a point roughly 2.5 km west of the Lodge a boggy path crosses the moor to hug the eastern shore of the Allt a'Chaoil-réidhe, passing Culra Lodge on the other bank, and eventually climbs to the bealach between Beinn Bheòil and Ben Alder. From the path rough slopes of boulders and heather lead west to the Short and Long

Leachas; both of these ridges provide natural mountain-routes at no more than Moderate standard, while the corries between and to the south have steep head-walls. Of the two, the Long Leachas has the better situations and in good winter conditions its narrow, upper part is an exhilarating scramble. Those seeking a walking route without the need to use hands for progress should cross the Allt a'Chaoil-réidhe by the bridge just north of Culra Lodge and follow the track to the Bealach Dubh, above which a course due south leads up easy slopes. The path continues west of the Bealach Dubh, skirting the western flanks of Ben Alder and improving as it descends from the Bealach Chumhann.

Again using the West Highland Line, a start can be made from Rannoch Station where 2 km east the 'Road to the Isles' turns in a northerly direction. Before reaching the Allt Gormag an indistinct path starts in a north-easterly direction at 435599 and grows ever fainter as it skirts the north of Lochan Sròn Smeur. Beyond the lochan only traces of the path occur and there are 3 km of rough going in an easterly direction, skirting south of recent afforestation and north of Lochan Loin nan Donnlaich, before a good track heading north is joined at 479617. This second track—an ancient route shown on Roy's Map of 1755—commences at the west end of Loch Rannoch and, being shorter and without the interruption effecting the other approach, may be preferable particularly to those arriving by car. A bus service between Kinloch Rannoch and Rannoch Station meets the north-bound, morning train and saves 11 km of road walking for those wanting to use the continuous track. However the moor-land area between the two lochans is rich in bird-life (herons seen feeding at the easterly lochan, both redshanks and green-shanks seen, grey wagtail and dippers also) which in spring makes the path through the glacial breach occupied by Lochan Sròn Smeur the more interesting. Beyond the junction a view of great splendour steadily unfolds with the length of Loch Ericht stretching into the distance and above it scarped slopes to the east and the unrelenting angle of those to the west beneath Sròn Coire na h'Iolaire are redolent of the glacier that oversteepened these walls, down-cutting by as much as 400 m. Beneath the bridge over the Cam Criochan slabs of pink granite form summer swimming pools that, in spring flood are invisible for this burn drains a vast shelf of saturated peat to the east of Sgòr

Gaibhre and Sgòr Choinnich. Once over the bridge the track dwindles to a path skirting afforestation, past which it fades altogether. For the next 2 km one wanders through an idyllic setting of Scots Pine forming open woodland, that is crowned by the view through the trees of Ben Alder and Sròn Coire na h'Iolaire. Alder Bay and Ben Alder Cottage add a hint of peace to heighten the grandeur of this scene.

At one time this corner held a small community and the diligent searcher will find rickles of stone amongst the bracken. When this hamlet died is not known but it must have been long before the pre-war inundation of the track along which pony-carts used to be driven from Dalwhinnie. The raising of the water level took place when Loch Ericht was dammed and its waters impounded to feed the turbines of the Grampian Electricity Supply Company, which in the 1930's was the first Scottish producer of hydro-electric power for public consumption.

Above the bay a faint path leads up north to the Bealach Breabag and an ascent of roughly 300 m brings easy slopes to the left, that lead on to a southerly ridge. Higher still the ridge bends north-west, flattens, and becomes better defined, skirting the rim of the Garbh Choire that in most winters carries enormous cornices. In summer Ben Alder's huge summit plateau is a fascinating place. Both ptarmigan and dotterel breed amongst the wilderness of granite boulders and moss campion favours the gravelly clearings along the western slopes. Then the sub-arctic climate promotes the phenomenon known as polygons, which is associated with perma-frost, where frost action extrudes stones into an occasionally recognisable pattern. When these extrusions do occur with regular form, there will be a central area of small stones surrounded by a polyagonal wall of larger stones. This outer wall can appear as a startlingly symmetrical design. With time enough for a careful search examples can be found on the flat ground west of the cairn: one such was measured at 130 cm diameter with the larger stones having a maximum dimension of 23 cm.

Little climbing has been recorded on Ben Alder and its rock features are, with one exception, lacking in a sufficiency of continuous and clean crag. This exception lies in a large, complex crag of quartz-feldspar facing east and north-east above

151

the southern end of Lochan a'Bhealaich Bheithe. It is known as the South Buttress of the Garbh Choire and although only one route has been recorded, there are undoubtedly other lines to be climbed. Facing north of east and low down on the buttress is a wall of c. 100 m split by two chimneys. The right-hand chimney gave the following route:

Uncle's Chimney   90 m   Very Difficult
Climbed in three pitches, each 30 m. First pitch partly on the right wall; second, involving an awkward chockstone, up the middle; third, the hardest, again partly on the right wall. There are good belays, the rock is sound after the first 8 m and the standard is sustained throughout.

However in winter its eastern corries and huge north face offer superb mountaineering. In the westernmost corner of the Garbh Choire a straightforward gully of Grade I standard makes a pleasant route while to its right an obvious ramp trends rightward up the open face to finish on steeper ground—the easiest line hereabouts would be of Grade II standard. Further right still the head-wall steepens yet more and in Garbh-choire Beag, though no definite lines present themselves, the uppermost 30 m are very steep indeed. On the north side of Ben Alder a hanging-valley indents deeply into the summit plateau, beneath a shallow depression separating the top above Garbh-choire Beag from the summit plateau. At the back of this corrie two snow gullies of Grade I standard are easily found and high on the west wall a vertical ice-fall often forms: the easiest line to its foot and escape above should provide a hard route of at least 100 m. Within this corrie, as on the external, bounding walls, there is scope for exploration. Further west a great, open face of rock looms above the path to the Bealach Dubh and has retained an enigmatic air despite the attention of several explorers. Certainly it is too broken to satisfy a taste for pure rock-climbing, but when plastered with old snow, for it appears to carry insufficient drainage for ice to form in any quantity, the potential for serious mountaineering is very attractive and will contain a stronger element than usual of exploration. A good view of the face can be had from the south-western slopes of Sgor Iutharn (unnamed on O.S. Sheet 42 First Series, 1:50,000—GR 490743), and from this viewpoint a series of diagonal weaknesses can be seen rising from right to left: in winter these terraces are not easy ground and escape along them is interrupted by slabby tongues of rock.

In winter, when even the excellent track from Dalwhinnie can take hours of toil through deep snow, Ben Alder shares with the deeper recesses of the Cairngorms, a quality of genuine remoteness. When winter storms blow here, and they seem as fierce in the long glens as on the top, the strongest party will be taxed.

In contrast should be set the prospect of a summer excursion to Loch Ossian. For many the delightfully picturesque situation of the wooden Youth Hostel—once a boat-house—on a promontory at the head of the loch, makes it the best of its kind in Britain—and of a wider field judging by the number of Continentals who return year after year. Some come to wander the hills but many have further interest in the flora and fauna, which in the latter case has great variety for such high land. With the mixed woodland of indigenous birch and a variety of mature, exotic conifers—the latter planted with fringes of hardwoods and flowering shrubs of azalea and rhododendrons under the plan of a forestry pioneer, Sir John Stirling Maxwell—providing food and shelter, there is an attractive mix of bird-life. Many of the common waders and passerines breed in the area, several ducks, game birds and birds of prey can be seen. Over 100 different species have been observed about the loch and the surrounding hills; golden plover keening over the slopes of Carn Dearg; heron fishing the shallows at the east end of the loch; redpoll, twite, siskin and other finches feeding in trees; and the distinctive mew of the buzzard has been heard, again over Carn Dearg. When Sir John Stirling Maxwell bought Corrour Estate in 1890 only the birch wood on the southern shore of the Loch provided shelter, but a year later he had started his experiments with the noble fir, larch, western hemlock and with the eventual groundrock of afforestation in Scotland—the sitka spruce. A memorial to this pioneer can be seen on a plaque inset in a granite boulder at the east end of the loch.

At this same east end of the loch, or better still walking down beside the Uisge Labhair, there is a disturbing sense of something awry in the landform: some may wonder at the sluggish meander of the River Ossian and the way it cuts through almost a lip of ground; others puzzle at the sudden turn north of the straight-

153

coursed Uisge Labhair. It is considered that at one time the Uisge Labhair drained into Loch Ossian and that the two flowed on into the Loch Treig basin. Later glaciation deepened Strath Ossian so that it captured the Uisge Labhair and, left morainic material to block Loch Ossian's western outlet.

Many of the lochans on the fringe of Rannoch Moor have a plentiful stock of small brown trout—Loch na Sheallaig is one such case—and for those spending some time in the area, a fishing rod would be almost as useful as a Primus stove.

Beinn Bheòil (1016 m), Sròn Coire na h'Iolaire (953 m)

This long spine of a hill has a splendid position cut off abruptly to the east by Loch Ericht and to the west by the trench containing the Loch a'Bhealaiche Bheithe. Its summit ridge carries clear evidence in granite erratics of the thickness of the ice that flowed north from the Rannoch ice-cap and ground out these two trenches. On the moor to the north one of these erratics is so nicely balanced on a plaque of schistose rock—itself planed by glacial action—that it can be rocked with one hand. Climbed from the north there are splendid views across to the Short and Long Leachas jutting out into the moor; further south the great eastern wall of Ben Alder is in full view; and the bealach between the two tops is a good position from which to study the South Buttress of the Garbh Choire. Sròn Coire na h'Iolaire (the nose of the eagle's corrie) is well-named as both eagles and hen harriers have been frequently sighted quartering the ground below this top. Descent west from the bealach between the two tops is down steep slopes of boulder and scree.

The Fara (910 m) (properly Am Faradh—the ladder)

The last top in this area lies in the north-east corner and is very accessible from Dalwhinnie. There can be few hills with such a great length of ridge above 800 m and roughly 7 km are spent walking on the easiest possible ground between the Fara and its far-flung outliers Meall Cruaidh (896 m) and Meall Leac na Sguabaich (843 m). The continuous view to the south-west is superb—the great through routes of An Lairig and the Bealach Dubh; the full length of Loch Ericht; and the corries and ridges of Aonach Beag and Ben Alder. Its great length would save the Fara from ever being described as nondescript but views from its ridge lift it quite out of the ordinary.

Also out of the ordinary is the great rift of Dirc Mhor (the great slash) that cuts into the Fara's northern flank. It was first brought to the attention of mountaineers by the landscape artist Colin Phillip and Harold Raeburn was quick to investigate. He found a remarkable cleft of 400 ft depth, with savage cliffs on either side but finer on the east and floored with a jungle of boulders and an abundance of ferns making the holes between the boulders difficult to see. Curiously there is no record of a second visit by Raeburn, though he recommended it; however the description stands and while the defile is easily enough reached by following the Allt an t'Sluic for 5 km almost to its head, progress along its bed is necessarily slow and cautious. It was not until 1966 that the first route on the sound granite buttresses was recorded: it was on the largest buttress on the east wall.

Sentinel Rock—Holy Smoke   90 m   Very Severe
Start just above and to the right of the lowest rocks in the lowest of three grassy alcoves leading on to the buttress. Climb a short wall, then move right across a slab and up over two large blocks to a ledge. Climb a corner on the left then move left along a ledge out on to the wall of the buttress and up to belay on small ledge on a slab (27 m). Up the left edge of the corner above to a prominent roof, left along a ledge to a large block, then hand-traverse up and rightwards until a narrow ledge leads rightwards. Go straight up then left to a slab and follow the crest to the top (38 m).
A. McKeith and party, August 1966.

Transport and Accommodation

The early morning train for Fort William has had a departure time from Glasgow of 6.00 am for two decades and more. However minor alterations occasionally appear in the timetable and it is worthwhile using British Rail's current publication. There is a bus service between Pitlochry and Kinloch Rannoch (tel. 0796-2290) and another between Kinloch Rannoch and

Rannoch Station (tel. 088 22 348). Dalwhinnie can be reached either by rail or by express coach service (tel. 0324 23901 or 031-556 2515). At Dalwhinnie and Rannoch Station there are good hotels but, apart from the Youth Hostel at Loch Ossian and two bothies, the interior is bare. Neither bothy—one at Culra Lodge best reached from Dalwhinnie and the other at Alder Bay best reached from the west end of Loch Rannoch— can be used during the stalking season from early August to late October, and outside that period they have become so popular that it is worth restating the policy of the Mountain Bothies Association, that these bothies are left open and maintained for use by small parties staying overnight. Any party of more than two hoping to spend more than one night should ideally telephone 052 82 224 for Culra and 088 23 207 for Ben Alder Cottage. The Youth Hostel is also heavily used and a written booking is advised.

References

Diadem Compendium 1982, W. H. Murray. Undiscovered Scotland for a paean to Ben Alder in Chapter 19.

Ben Alder Cottage

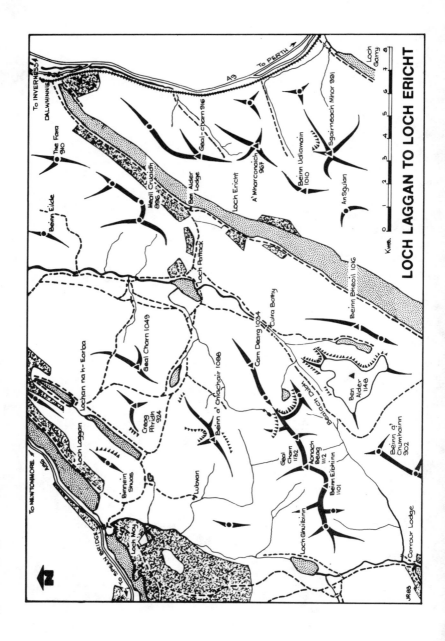

LOCH LAGGAN TO LOCH ERICHT

12

Loch Ossian
to Loch Laggan

*Stob Coire Sgriodain (976 m)
*Chno Dearg (1047 m)
  Meall Garbh (977 m)
*Beinn na Lap (937 m)
*Beinn Eibhinn (1100 m)
*Aonach Beag (1114 m)
*Geal Charn (1132 m) 470746
*Beinn a'Chlachair (1088 m)
*Creag Pitridh (924 m)
*Geal Charn (1049 m) 504812
  Carn Dearg (1034 m) 504764

Those hills in the interior of this area share with Ben Alder a
decided air of remoteness and even those relatively accessible
from Loch Laggan have a sense of being cut off by the barriers
of Lochan na h'Earba and the two Binneins, Shuas and Shios.
Three lochs form pronounced boundaries—Laggan, Treig and
Ossian—with the great divide between Ben Alder and Aonach
Beag and the River Pattack closing the ring. Enclosed within are
the awesome glacial trench of Strath Ossian, a fine crag on Chno
Dearg and a complement of stalkers' hill paths and estate tracks
greater than in any other area of the Central Highlands. Again as
with Ben Alder the sense of remoteness is preserved by use of
the West Highland Line to Corrour Halt, although there are
three points of access from the Spean-Laggan valley, and,
Dalwhinnie makes another, more distant starting point.

Stob Coire Sgriodain, Chno Dearg, Meall Garbh

These three hills make a natural round from Fersit, while for an

159

extra 3 km one can include the intriguing Garbh-bheinn in the traverse from Corrour Halt to Tulloch Station.

Fersit is a backwater that appears little effected by the adjacent, massive works of man in the dams at Loch Treig and Loch Laggan. The single-track road to it winds through hummocky ground crossing the Spean, the Allt Làire, and the River Treig in little more than 3 km. The few houses mingle with straggling Scots Pine and, birch follow the Allt Laire down to the road. Nevertheless it is not difficult to imagine the enormous forces that once went to make the general shape of this idyllic corner. For 10,000 years ago a glacier, major enough to have down-cut the fault-line now occupied by Loch Treig by 550 m, was forcing its great bulk through the constriction now straddled by the dam. In retreat this glacier left some classic examples of deposition in the cones of sand and gravel clustered about the road-end, and had carried some boulders of Rannoch granite as far as Tulloch. Where the road climbs from Inverlair Bridge, there is one of the clearest examples known in Scotland of those melt-holes left by stranded masses of ice: in Gaelic it is called Slochd a'Mheirlich (the robber's pit) and it is easily seen at the side of the road at 337801.

Lochs Treig and Laggan were dammed in the 1930's to provide water-power for the turbines of the British Aluminium Company and a 24 km tunnel now carries water from both lochs beneath the hills to Fort William. The damming of Loch Treig raised the high-water level by 33 ft, potentially inundating the old level of the railway track and an extensive section complete with a tunnel (at 347764) had to be relaid higher up the hillside.

The northern slopes of Stob Coire Sgriodain make heavy going over bouldery ground, though *roches moutonnées* and glacially-scoured slabs provide distraction and there is a splendid view from the top with the fiord-like Loch Treig curving west at its head and leading the eye to Binnein Mor and Beag. There are two other distinct tops to the south-east before a longer descent to the dip in line for Meall Garbh. This dip appears to gather unusually deep drifts of snow and, in poor visibility, is broad enough to be confusing as is its proximity to the dip between Meall Garbh and Chno Dearg, only 20 m above. Chno Dearg offers its own fine view across the flats holding Loch Ghuilbinn and backed by Beinn a'Chlachair, while behind again is the prominent gap occupied by Lochan na h'Earba and the diminutive cone of Binnein Shuas. Easy slopes lead north for return to Fersit but it is worthwhile keeping due north and turning to the east of Creag Dubh (607 m) partly to meet the path from Strath Ossian, but more to see the double rampart of terminal moraines that starts just above the path and curves round to follow the edge of the forest and the course of the Allt Loraich.

The traverse of these tops from Corrour to Tulloch follows the old drove route alongside the railway and turns up onto Garbh-bheinn at the foot of the Allt Luib Ruairidh. There is little or no trace here of the stance that once catered for the drovers who had brought their cattle and sheep over 13 km or so of difficult ground from the previous night's lodging under Sgurr Innse. Garbh-bheinn is notable for the multitude of perched blocks that litter its long south-west ridge and give rise to its Gaelic name—the rough hill; and, in an area where fine views abound, that to the west toward the head of Glen Nevis is outstanding. This route is recommended as a ski tour, and in this northerly direction as the northern slopes of Chno Dearg carry a quantity of snow unusually large for their altitude.

Creagan Coire nam Cnàmh

This crag has previously been written as 'Chno Dearg; Meall Garbh; East Face' and though its Gaelic name is not used on Sheet 41 O.S. Second Series 1:50,000, it is less clumsy. The crag is at 374729 and is composed of quartz-feldspar-granulite. Though not a major crag there are yet no crampon scratches here and ice builds up readily from a wealth of drainage and seep. On a dry summer's day or one of little snow but good frost, the quickest route is on a bearing from Fersit to the dip between Chno Dearg and Meall Garbh. In most other conditions the hill path from Fersit into Strath Ossian and then another leading west up the left bank of the Allt Feith Thuill makes easier going. When fresh snow lies on the hill this path, though twice the length of the direct route, can be quicker and it does have the advantage of a clear view of the crag during the last 2 km. At the foot and centre of the crag is an obvious inverted 'V' formation: the left-hand leg is the start of 'Watcher's Wall' which traverses right and under the giant chockstone and cave at

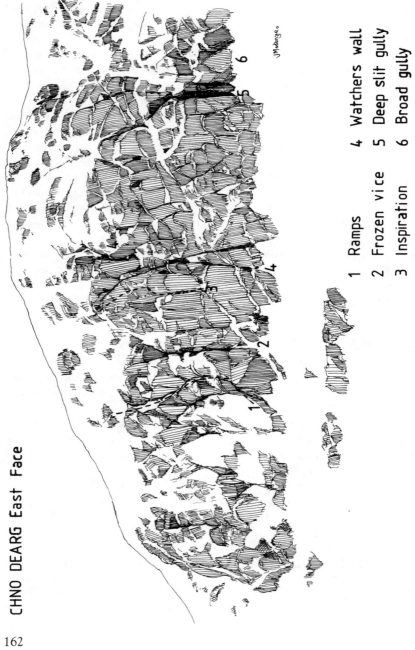

CHNO DEARG East Face

1 Ramps   4 Watchers wall
2 Frozen vice 5 Deep slit gully
3 Inspiration 6 Broad gully

84. *Starting down the Long Leachas*   *Peter Hodgkiss*

85. *Sgòr Choinnich and Sgòr Gaibhre from the north.*   *Peter Hodgkiss*

86.   Loch Ossian and Leum Uilleam from the slopes of Beinn Eibhinn.   Peter Hodgkiss

87.   The Bealach Dubh from the east: Sgòr Iutharn's 'Lancet Edge' to the right and Ben Alder to the left.
                                                                                        W. Mockridge

88.   Strath Ossian from the north.   *Peter Hodgkiss*

89.   The vast plateau of Creag Meagaidh from Chno Dearg. Beinn a' Chaorainn to the left.
Peter Hodgkiss

90. *Creag Pitridh, Geal Charn, and Beinn a' Chlachair (from left to right); late afternoon.*
Peter Hodgkiss

91.   *Storm clouds crossing Loch Laggan toward the cone of Binnein Shuas.*

Peter Hodgkiss

92.   The parallel roads of Glen Roy. Brae Roy Lodge in the foreground; Carn Bhrunachain behind.   Peter Hodgkiss

93.   The cliffs of Coire Ardair, 1951.   G. S. Johnstone

94.   Beinn a' Chaorainn's east face.   D. Green

the apex of the 'V'; the deep gash of the right-hand leg and the continuation in a groove above the chockstone is unclimbed in summer or winter. For diagram see page 162.

Watcher's Wall   120 m   Severe
Climb left-hand leg of inverted 'V' at bottom-centre and traverse right before cave to easy ledge. Along ledge reach foot of deep-cut chimney, which climb to small, deep cave with chockstone belay (25 m). Continue in chimney for 12 m to grass below only obvious weakness in steep wall above. Belay. Climb line of weakness, a chimney groove, for 2 m then horizontally right for 8 m to another chimney which climb past awkward overhanging projection to easy ground.
P. Tranter and I. G. Rowe, October 1964.

Inspiration   125 m   Severe
50 m left of the left-hand leg a grassy ledge slants up right. Move along this for 35 m to split corner and up this for 8 m. Trend left to obvious corner which follow to grass and belays (30 m). More grass, then a large, obvious block and gain ridge on right (30 m). This steepens to form crux. Easy rocks beyond.
W. Fraser and A. Park, October 1964.

The Ramp   185 m   Grade III
This is the obvious left trending ramp cutting across the steep walls left of the main buttress. Access to the ramp is by a steep-angled rightwards traverse from the foot of the walls.
A. Wielochowski, February 1976.

The Frozen Vice   110 m   Grade IV
This route climbs the deep chimney above the foot of the grassy ledge used in *Inspiration*. Climb the steep, wide chimney and another above which narrows to a slit.
G. Thomas and A. Wielochowski, March 1976.

Broad Gully   150 m   Grade III
This is the broad gully right of the main buttress. Climb the introductory ice pitch which is always steep and interrupted at mid-height by a snow bay. Straghtforward snow slopes above.
J. Crowden and A. Wielochowski, April 1976.

Deep Slit Gully   140 m   Grade III

25 m left of *Broad Gully* is a deep, narrow gully. Climb to less pronounced and left-tranding ramp and grooves above.
A. Wielochowski, February 1976.

Beinn na Lap (937 m)

Few hills in such a remote setting can be so easily climbed from a railway station. Leaving the train at Corrour Halt the old drove route follows beside the track to the foot of the south-westerly slopes at an altitude of 400 m, and above a ridge carpeted with dwarf vegetation and at the easiest of angles, leads to the top. Like other hills about the head of Loch Treig, there is a fine outlook and the contrast between the mountainous ridges to the west and the flat expanse of Rannoch Moor to the south deserves a clear day for its appreciation. From the top a long, low-angled ridge leads north-east over platelets of quartzite and above the profound cut to the north-west of a major fault-line that continues through Lochan na h'Earba: this extraordinary feature runs an almost geometrically straight course through the hills and gains only 50 m in the 4 km between the Ossian flats and the tiny Lochan Ruigh Phàil at its highest point. Where the ridge drops into the flats west of Strathossian House the underlying rock changes to granite as can be seen in the burn where good pools for swimming are ringed with boulders of pink and cream granite. Return from such a crossing is easily made by the excellent tracks through Strath Ossian and along the north side of Loch Ossian. The vast shelf of high ground to the east of the summit, containing Loch na Lap, should be avoided as it is a waste of poorly-drained peat-hags.

Strath Ossian's pronounced 'U' shape so indicative of glaciation, is perhaps best appreciated from the hills and to walk its length in poor weather can seem a dreary stretch. However from the bed of the strath it is still easy to picture the Ossian Glacier grinding north and polishing the two granite crags—both known as Creagan nan Nead—to either side at the mouth of the strath. Of these two crags, that to the east forming a nose above Strathossian House has been investigated and the climbing reported as poor; that on the west wall might better repay exploration but neither would provide climbs of any length nor match the quality of the adjacent crag on Chno Dearg.

Beinn Eibhinn (1100 m), Aonach Beag (1114 m), Geal Charn (1049), Sgor Iutharn (1014 m), Carn Dearg (1034 m)

These hills form one long and elevated ridge between Strath Ossian and Loch Pattack set at such great distance from both road and rail that they are not easily accessible for a day's outing. However, a fast-moving party not meeting any delaying factor such as fresh snow, can make the ascent of the three western tops in the 10 hours between trains from Corrour. At least 38 km would be involved in such a rush, leaving no time to explore the corries and ridges to the east and perhaps needing Wm. W. Naismith's regimen of 'young men eating their pieces on the move'. The south-westerly route onto Beinn Eibhinn is straightforward until the confusing area between the main summit and two minor tops—Mullach Choire nan Nead (921 m) 431734; Meall Ghlas Choire (922 m) 438729—neither of which is named on Sheet 42 O.S. First Series 1:50,000. There is however, no mistaking the almost square section of the narrow window (Uinneag a Ghlas Choire) between the last-named top and Beinn Eibhinn.

Another long approach, but one recommended for the views into the shapely northern corries, starts from the concrete bridge 8 km east of the Laggan dam. A forestry track starts here and runs through to Strath Ossian but a path on the east of the Amhainn Ghuilbinn should be followed. This leads across Meall Ardruigh to Lùbvan and thence up the course of the Allt Cam to the foot of Aonach Beag's north-north-west ridge. Either it or a parallel ridge to Beinn Eibhinn make pleasant routes, and in good winter conditions an easy snow climb but with a steep finish can be had from the corrie almost enclosed between the two ridges (Coire a'Chàrra Mhóir). The north ridge of Geal Charn steepens to a nose at the plateau rim and while the nose can be circumvented, the avoiding line for descent is not easily found in poor visibility from the featureless plateau. In winter those without experience of snow and ice climbing would probably not be comfortable in descending by this route.

There are some ideal camping sites along this approach but the flats at the head of the Allt Cam are subjected to strong winds.

The third and longest approach is that by the estate tracks

leading to Loch Pattack from either Dalwhinnie or Kinloch Laggan and a traverse of the three tops from this junction makes a fine winter expedition. To walk in beside the Pattack is the pleasanter route with fine waterfalls at Linn of Pattack and, a little beyond at a bridge, there is an abandoned channel worn out of solid rock. From a large shed south of Loch Pattack a boggy path leads south-west, and after 4 km a bridge across the Allt a'Chaoil-réidhe should be crossed. Those favoured with a clear winter's day will see ahead the route up Sgor Iutharn—a sharp ridge known as the 'Lancet Edge', that is narrow enough to require care. Steep ground sweeps down on either side of the ridge and the view left and right—to the hanging valley on Ben Alder's north face and to Loch an Sgòir fed by a tracery of waterfalls—is very fine indeed. By contrast the ground between Sgor Iutharn and Geal Charn is easy going and the latter's summit plateau is surprisingly extensive and well irrigated by snow-fields that last into summer. Composed of mica-schist and producing luxuriant summer grass, this top is favourite grazing for deer.

In poor visibility it is worthwhile taking a careful bearing for the steep, narrow ridge leading down to the saddle known as Diollaid a'Chàirn. Many parties trend too far right and follow a parallel ridge until they find themselves peering down the crags above Loch an Sgòir. Carn Dearg can seem anti-climatic after such interest, but in poor weather there is a tendency for it to be free of cloud when its massed neighbours to the west have allowed no view.

Beinn a'Chlachair (1088 m), Geal Charn (1049 m), Creag Pitridh (924 m)

Another natural grouping is formed by the hills between Lochan na h'Earba and An Lairig but, in this case, one readily accessible from the A86 to the north. Nearest access is by the bridge at 432830 from where a path joins the estate track to Lochan na h'Earba. A hill path continues from the west of the Lochan to a bealach central to the three hills and overlooking a bleak stretch of water to the east—Loch a'Bhealaich Leamhainn. This path, as with most in the Ardverikie Forest, is well engineered and still fairly well drained: it makes better walking than the northern flank of Beinn a'Chlachair which in its lower half can be very wet. As the Gaelic name—Hill of the Mason—suggests, the hill is littered with boulders, which on the east-north-east shoulder and on the upper cone are frequently of regular proportions. The shoulder terminates sharply to the east in a schist crag above the loch, but it appears too broken and loose for climbing. Also disappointing in climbing terms, though impressive from a distance, is the northern corrie.

A further path leads to the bealach between Creag Pitridh and Geal Charn. It branches from the main path between the hills at the apex of a long zig-zag, engineered to avoid a gully beneath the south-west nose of Geal Charn. Even with the presence of this path, the bealach is a confusing place in thick weather and is one of those very rare places not accurately drawn by the Ordnance Survey on their Sheet 42, First Series 1:50,000 map. The path actually ascends the western slope of Geal Charn and remains 20 m above and 200 m east of the bealach before dropping quite sharply to the north.

Geal Charn once more conveniently known—in view of its namesake across the An Lairig—as Mullach Coire an Iubhair, is largely composed of lime-rich mica-schist and produces some rare Alpines on craggy ground protected by its steepness from grazers and also from the rapacity of that other plunderer—the Victorian collector. Purple saxifrage blooms hereabout in early spring and Alpine hawkweed has also been seen. The hills of the Ardverikie Forest seem also to have a particularly rich and varied crop of lichens and at one time dyers of tweed produced some of their less common colours (known as 'crottles' from the Gaelic word *crotal*) from lichen gathered on these hills.

For those returning to Kinloch Laggan the narrow north-east spur of Geal Charn provides a splendid route with a little scrambling low down and leads to another good path descending to the Pattack.

Binnein Shuas (746 m)

Lying between Loch Laggan and Lochan na h'Earba, and almost a peninsula, is a strip of land carrying Binnein Shuas and Binnein Shios. Both hills offer outstanding views up and down the length of the Spean-Laggan valley and both are easily reached by their south-west ridges. Binnein Shuas carries a major crag of pegmatite on its east face which lay unexplored until the 1960's: it now has a host of excellent rock-climbs, a selection of which are described with two line diagrams and several photographs in A. C. Stead's *Rock and Ice Climbs in Lochaber and Badenoch*. This crag is blessed with largely sound rock and, being at such low altitude, offers comfortable climbing when the high mountain cliffs are out of condition.

Transport and Accommodation

Remarks at the end of the last chapter concerning transport apply here also and there is an additional bothy that can be used outside the stalking season. This is Blackburn Bothy which is 2 km north of Loch Pattack (544 817).

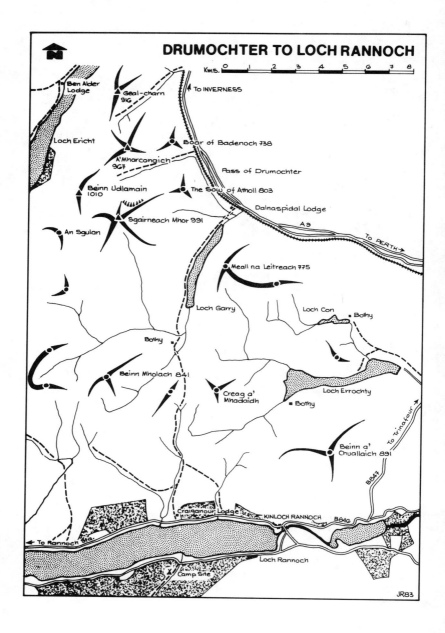

DRUMOCHTER TO LOCH RANNOCH

Kms. 0 1 2 3 4 5 6 7 8

Ben Alder Lodge

Geal-charn 916

To INVERNESS

Loch Ericht

Boar of Badenoch 738

A'Mharcongich 967

Pass of Drumochter

Beinn Udlamain 1010

The Sow of Atholl 803

Dalnaspidal Lodge

Sgairneach Mhor 991

A9

To PERTH →

An Sgulan

Meall na Leitreach 775

Loch Garry

Loch Con

Bothy

Bothy

Beinn Mholach 841

Creag a' Mhadaidh

Loch Errochty

Bothy

Beinn a' Chuallaich 891

To Trinafour →

B847

Craiganour Lodge

KINLOCH RANNOCH

B846

← To Rannoch

Loch Rannoch

Camp Site

JR83

170

13

Drumochter

Geal Charn (917 m)
A'Mharconaich (975 m)
Beinn Udlamain (1010 m)
Sgairneach Mhor (991 m)
  Meall na Leitreach (775 m)
  Beinn Mholach (841 m)
  Beinn a'Chuallaich (891 m)
  Stob an Aonaich Mhoir (855 m)

This small group of hills lies in the south-eastern corner of the
Central Highlands and with its heather-clad eastern slopes and
flat rolling plateau seems more akin to the Cairngorms. However
the Scottish 'Khyber Pass' of Drumochter (Druim uachdar—the
highest ridge) acts as a dividing line and the watershed of
Scotland is appropriately not far north where the rivers Pattack
and Mashie drain the same hill but then turn west and east
respectively. Another boundary is the great length of Loch
Ericht and, looking on the slopes dropping steeply into the loch
beneath Geal Charn, it is easy to imagine the depth of the glacier
that gouged out the fault line here to give the loch a depth of
150 m. To the south the northern shore of Loch Rannoch and
the road from Bridge of Ericht to the A9 form the base of a
triangle containing few distinctive hills but a great southern area
of bad-lands where the ground rises and falls imperceptively
over a waste of hummock, bog and meandering burns. The Pass
of Drumochter, bleak and treeless, is a gloomy place in anything
but the best of weather, however there is interest in the litter of
glacial moraines at the entrance to Coire Dhomhain and again at
Dalnaspidal. At the latter place the glacier flowing north from
the Loch Garry basin, as Geike tell us 'split upon the summit of
the Pass and sent one branch into Glen Garry, the other into
Glen Truim'. In most winters, with its height, drifting snow
closes the road to traffic, but this same height offers reliable

mountain ski-ing and has encouraged recent investigation into the installation of ski-lifts. Early drovers must have found the Pass if not the most hostile in terms of height, the most congested, for two major routes from the north and the north-west converged here. Bishop Forbes in 1723 found eight droves, totalling 1200 beasts, at the Daiwhinnie stance, another drove covering a mile's length in the Pass itself and a further drove of 300 grazing at the head of Loch Garry.

The high hills are gathered in the northerly corner and with their easy terrain and a starting point at 450 m above sea-level can be traversed easily in a day. For such a round the best starting point is near the summit of Drumochter at the entrance to Coire Dhomhain, from where an obvious circuit winds over Sgairneach Mhor, Beinn Udlamain and A' Mharconaich and is faulted only by the need to turn north for the ascent of Geall Charn and the retracing of steps back over A'Mharconaich. Navigation is also straightforward with the small exception of a series of dog-leg movements between Sgairneach Mhor and Beinn Udlamain, but the clear drawing on Sheet 42 O.S. First Series 1:50,000 map make these obvious. Both the Sow of Atholl (762 m) and the Boar of Badenoch (738 m) are easily included in this round and north of the bealach between the former and Sgairneach Mhor, there is a fine gorge that provides a scramble on a dry summer's day. In an area where heather grows in profusion, the Sow is singular in having the only site in Scotland of the Norwegian blue heather (Menziesia). But perhaps the most notable feature of these hills is the view that they provide of the Ben Alder massif, and in this respect Geal Charn has the edge: it can be reached quickly from Balsporran Cottages by a path that carries through thick heather on the north side of the Allt Coire Fhar. From this path a group of giants seem to be marching parallel along the skyline above, but they are nothing more than a series of cairns 3 m high. If return is made to the north and over Creagan Mor, it is well worth diverting west to the edge of Creag Dubh, from where the great length of Loch Ericht and the vast corries of Ben Alder and Aonach Beag provide one of the finest views in Scotland.

South of the Pass at Dalnaspidal where, sadly there is no longer a railway station, an ancient track, shown on Roys Map of 1755, runs alongside Loch Garry and through to Loch

Rannoch. Apart from being a pleasant long-distance walk, it offers the only reasonable access to **Beinn Mholach** in the heart of a waste-land. **Meall na Leitreach** above Loch Garry can also be included in this route, but between its southern spur—Sron nam Faiceachan—and the bridge over the Allt na Duinish, there is 1 km of marsh that can be very wet. At the southern end of the track the east fork leading to Annat should be taken, as the other fork runs through the private grounds of Craiganour Lodge. A hillock between these forks carries an exposure of intrusive igneous rock known as Creagan Odhar, that runs for 1 km in a remarkably straight line and shows the predominant grain of the rock in this area.

There is a bus service between Pitlochry and Kinloch Rannoch and the limited stop service from Pitlochry to Inverness will set down at Dalnaspidal given prior warning.

West of the Garry to Rannoch track there is an area which, particularly in its southern half, will attract only the confirmed seeker of solitude. Its featureless plateau of tussocky bog is cut by shallow glens and meandering burns, and carries some extensive plots of afforestation, the most recent of which is not shown on Sheet 42 First Series O.S. 1:50,000 map: it covers a triangle between Loch Rannoch, the Killichonan Burn and the Aulich Burn. One path runs through the area, from Killichonan to Coire Bhachdaidh Lodge on Loch Ericht and further west a private road runs from Bridge of Ericht to the dam at the foot of Loch Ericht.

That remote hill **Stob an Aonaich Mhoir**, can be reached by either path or road but both involve a minimum distance of 28 km and rough, wet going.

Beinn a'Chuallaich is easily ascended from the south by way of a ridge, starting from the roadside 3 km east of Kinloch Rannoch, and also from the north where above Trinafour steep slopes clad with indigenous woodland lead to a spur, Meall Ban. There is a series of short crags on another southern spur of Beinn a'Chuallaich. They are known as Craig Varr and can be reached in five minutes from a point on the road 1 km east of Kinloch Rannoch. Twelve routes of from 30 m to 50 m length and varying from Very Difficult to Very Severe, have been recorded and all are detailed in Dave Cuthbertson's guide *Creag Dubh and Craig-a-Barns*, SMC 1983.

References

Robert Forbes Journal, J. B. Craven's 1886 edition.
The Scenery of Scotland, A. Geike (O.P.), 1901.
Scottish Mountains on ski, M. Slesser.

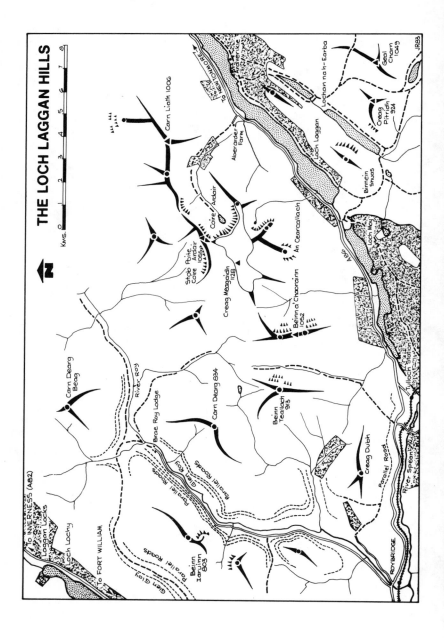

THE LOCH LAGGAN HILLS

14

The Loch Laggan Hills:
Creag Meagaidh
and Glen Roy

Beinn Iaruinn (800 m) 296900
Carn Dearg (815 m) (Glean Eachach) 349967
Carn Dearg (768 m) (north of Glen Roy) 345887
Carn Dearg (834 m) (south of Glen Roy) 357948
Beinn Teallach (913 m) 361859
*__Beinn a'Chaorainn__ (1052 m) 386851
*__Creag Meagaidh__ (1130 m) 418875
An Cearcallach (993 m) 422854
Puist Coire Ardair (1070 m) 436873
Meall Coire Choille-rais (1027 m) 433862
*__Stob Poite Coire Ardair__ (1053 m) 429889
*__Carn Liath__ (1006 m) 472903

This vast area is contained within a triangle made between the
Great Glen, Glen Spean and the Corrieyairack track. Because of
the multiplicity of Carn Deargs and because of the complex
topography of Creag Meagaidh itself, Ordnance Survey grid
references are given.

Creag Meagaidh

When seen from a distance the plateau-like nature of the Creag
Meagaidh range is the overriding impression and it is only from
close at hand that one can appreciate the mountainous nature of
the great corries. Similarly only first-hand experience will give
an idea of the confusing twists to the ridges radiated by Creag
Meagaidh which in plan is somewhat akin to a Catherine-wheel.
Allied to these curving arms and deeply-cut corries, a summit

plateau of greater extent than is immediately clear from a 1:50,000 map, make Creag Meagaidh one of the most confusing hills, in navigational terms, in the Central Highlands; and piloting off the top in a winter storm is a more than usually serious business, as is evidenced by the number of parties who spend an unplanned night out at the head of Glen Roy. (That most devoted of mountaineers Wm. W. Naismith was quoted as remarking to Wm. Douglas, while they were groping their way to the summit, that 'if he had at that moment to choose between mountaineering and golf, then the former would go by the board': SMCJ, Vol. V, p. 126.)

. A traverse of all the tops from Aberarder Farm is a splendid outing of reasonable length and if started over **Carn Liath** gives ample opportunity to gaze at the unique architecture of Coire Ardair's head-wall. Beyond **Stob Poite Coire Ardair** (unnamed on Sheet 34 1:50,000 Second Series O.S. map) a sharp turn south drops steeply into 'The Window'—a key feature in winter descents after climbs in Coire Ardair, but one not found without the most careful of compass work. Very large cornices form on the ridge leading south-east from 'The Window', these mark the rim of the 'Inner Coire'—that is, the right-hand (north) flank of Coire Ardair, which is further recessed and on an upper level to the main face. The summit itself is oddly removed from the hub on a south-west ridge, and those on their first visit approaching from the south-east or north-east in anything but perfect visibility may doubt the presence of higher ground beyond the large cairn at 424878. In descending east over **Puist Coire Ardair** and **Sron a Choire** (1001 m) [repeatedly misprinted as Ghoire on O.S. maps], there are fine downward views into Coire Choille-rais and then over to the cliffs of Coire Ardair. It wants only a short diversion from the Puist to walk south-west to the twin tops of **An Cearcallach** and to retrace one's steps via **Meall Coire Choille-rais**.

An ascent of Creag Meagaidh alone can be made quickly, and with the best chance of finding the summit cairn in thick weather, up the long south ridge, but the first kilometre or so above Moy is of hag-ridden and badly drained ground.

Coire Ardair and its cliffs make an already interesting hill, one to rank with Ben Nevis and Lochnagar in the quality of its winter climbing. Indeed until the end of the last century the name

'Coire Ardair' was used by local people to cover the whole range (Mrs. Grant in her 'letters from the Mountains' refers to the range as 'lofty Corryarder'). While the cliffs can be viewed from various points on the surrounding horseshoe, the greatest impression will be made on those approaching by the path from Aberarder Farm. A little beyond the farm the path veers up hill and carries through the fringe of a fine birch wood—one of the few large stands of regenerative birch at such an altitude in the Central Highlands. From the last trees the remarkably ordered structure of buttresses and posts (gullies) comes into view and gives an added impression of grand scale. The three main posts and their accompanying pillars are all serious winter routes of 400 m length, though tolerance of vegetation, that was a secondary matter to Raeburn and J. H. B. Bell whose priorities were exploration, must accompany any approach to rock-climbing on the very steep mica schist. J. H. B. Bell observed that apart from their steepness, these crags possessed two habits inimical to the rock climber—'they form a fertile subsoil for lichens and other vegetation, and they abound in undercut faces and ledges which thin out and peter away into nothingness'. Bell's friend Wedderburn put it succinctly when he remarked that 'the faces would almost appear to be easier if they were turned upside down'.

There are only two winter routes that could be described as straightforward—Raeburn's Gully, 360 m, Grade I, slanting up left and to the left of Pinnacle Buttress, and Easy Gully, 450 m, Grade I, slanting up left from beneath the Post Face. Neither is easily located for descent as the upper portion of the Post Face and the plateau rim are lacking in identifiable features such as indented gully bays. Many of the harder routes finish up feature-less slopes of relatively easy angle, and unless the top of Raeburn's or Easy Gully has been positively identified a descent via 'The Window' is strongly advised.

The Inner Coire does provide several routes in the Grade II category but they retain a serious atmosphere in a high and remote setting. These routes and all other major routes are described in A. C. Stead's *Rock and Ice Climbs in Lochaber and Badenoch*, which is well illustrated with line diagrams and photographs.

Throughout the history of climbing on Creag Meagaidh there

have been repeated accounts, in impressive and more than coincidental numbers, of avalanches: Raeburn, J. H. B. Bell and W. H. Murray all had experience of the rushing snows beneath the chutes of the Posts and in modern times the frequency of reports increases. Explanation can be found in Coire Ardair's marginal position—open to the severity of the Continental weather systems and yet prone to the sudden thaws from the south-west; additionally its enclosed corrie beneath the gathering ground of the extensive summit plateau leads to vast accumulations of snow.

There is another climbing ground on Creag Meagaidh and one in a truly remote setting. It is in the crags above Loch Roy which either from the head of Glen Roy or via 'The Window' from Coire Ardair will take $3\frac{1}{2}$hr. This long approach could be shortened by sleeping at the open and rough bothy known as Luib-chonnal (394936). Most of the climbs so far recorded are on the north-east facing crags of Carn Dearg at 412895.

Carn Dearg

Wet Walk   120 m   Grade I
The left branch of the shallow double gully on the right-hand side of the buttress with a steep uncorniced section at the top.
B. J. G. Chambers and K. Schwartz, February 1972.

The Rough Ride   135 m   Grade II
The steep rightwards-trending chimney above and to the right of the lower part of the obvious deep-cut gully (The Spin). Follow chimney over bulge to ridge. Climb buttress edge above to plateau.
B. J. G. Chambers and K. Schwartz, February 1972.

The Spin   150 m   Grade I
The deepest-cut gully in the right-hand section of the buttress. Keep to right near top where huge cornice is smallest. Good situations.
B. J. G. Chambers and K. Schwartz, February 1972.

Midnight Crunch   165 m   Grade II
The pleasant gully curving between the broken centre wall on the left and the well defined buttress left of The Spin. Follow

gully with several short, steep ice pitches to snow ridge. Then left past rocks to cornice.
B. J. G. Chambers and K. Schwartz, February 1972

Big Red Van   210 m   Grade III
A good route on the broken central wall between the big gully on the left and Midnight Crunch on the right, closer to the latter. Go up short ice-gully to snow-field which leads to shallow steep ice-gully. Move from its top to short vertical pitch further right. From its top go left over steep ground to start of obvious rightwards-trending gully-ramp. Steep ice steps above lead to snow slope and cornice.
J. Mount and K. Schwartz, February 1972.

Directly above Loch Roy and facing due north, are the crags of Creag an Lochain (418890) and only one route has been recorded.

Loch Roy Gully   180 m   Grade IV
This route lies just right of the centre of Creag an Lochain, (grid ref. 417890) starting right of the lowest rocks and leads up into the obvious, very narrow chimney-gully (crux) near the top.
R. Schipper and J. Mount, February 1972.

There is ample scope for further exploration on both crags but with their tops at an altitude of c. 850 m, winter climbing conditions are much less reliable than in Coire Ardair.
In most winters Creag Meagaidh's corries and deeply incised glens harbour vast accumulations of snow and none more so than the south facing glen of the Moy Burn. For mountain skiers this makes a fine run, which with its dog-leg course can provide 6 km of ski-ing before the peat-hags above Moy.

Beinn a'Chaorainn (1052 m)

This hill has the form of a south-north spine with three distinct tops, and is joined to Creag Meagaidh in the north-east at a high bealach of 820 m (Bealach a'Bharnish). The centre top is the highest by a bare 2 m and throws down to the east a narrow ridge that makes a fine winter ascent. Recent afforestation covers the width of the southern approach and it is worthwhile using the Forestry track that commences half a kilometre east of the

Laggan dam wall at Roughburn. From the point where the track turns east and west it is better in ascending to turn on the west, the spur of Meall Clachaig. If good winter conditions prevail the long detour east on the track through the forest—in order to reach the Allt na h'Uamha—is worthwhile for the quality of the east ridge.

Beinn Teallach (913 m)

The Forestry track starting at Roughburn makes the best route to this hill and the Allt a'Chaorainn can be crossed dry-shod by following at the same level from the end of the track's east branch to a footbridge. Above, the southern flank offers easy going though there are steep northern and eastern corries beneath the summit. From this top there is a splendid view down the length of Loch Treig which appears lacking in a sea-ward exit, so fiord-like is its character.

Ascent of the other four tops, grouped around the head of Glen Roy, has a special interest, for few people can fail to be intrigued by the 'Parallel Roads' clearly seen on both sides when driving up the glen. Beinn Iaruinn and the three Carn Deargs are approached most easily from the public road reaching Brae Roy Lodge. The more northerly pair of Carn Deargs make a pleasant round from Turret Bridge with a good track running into the open mouth of Glen Turret, above which a 'parallel road' at 350 m can be followed north into Gleann Eachach. If the northernmost top is ascended first—by way of Teanga Mhor (the great tongue)—then descent from the sister peak will provide (weather permitting) a particularly clear view of the 'Parallel Roads'. Beyond Turret Bridge a second bridge crosses the Roy and offers the best approach to the southernmost Carn Dearg over knolly ground. Very steep slopes of grass and heather lead directly to Beinn Iaruinn from the bridge at the foot of Coire an t-Seilich: a more easy-angled slope up the north-east ridge starts beyond Turret Bridge.

The origin of the 'Parallel Roads' was first correctly proposed by the Swiss glaciologist Louis Agassiz in 1840—before that time Fingal of Gaelic legend was confidently asserted as the ancient engineer. Later in the 19th century T. F. Jamieson carried out a great deal of research and the general definition that he gave in 1863 remains little altered. The roads are in fact strands remaining from lakes pounded by the great glaciers from the Treig basin, from Ben Nevis and from further west that met in Glen Spean. Such clear terraces remain because these lakes formed during the last period of glaciation in Scotland, known as the Loch Lomond Advance, that began its retreat 10,000 years ago. As can be seen from the clear drawing on Sheet 34 of the O.S. Second Series, there are three distinct altitudes for the terraces and these represent the three water-levels maintained between the uncovering of successively lower outlet-bealachs as the glaciers retreated and the ice-dams lowered. Again the Ordnance Survey show on their Sheet 34 these outlets—marked as 'col': that at 410943 marks the upper level of 350 m, when the conglomeration of glaciers in the Spean Valley spread east beyond the present Laggan Dam and pushed ice-lobes half-way up Glen Roy; that at 337835 marks the first stage in retreat when the dam across Gleann Glas Dhoire was breached and an outlet of 326 m flowed east into the Spean Valley. While the 'road' marked 261 and 262 m represents a further stage of glacial retreat when the ice dam held in one great lake filling Glen Roy and the Spean/Laggan Valley.

Those wishing to read more about the Parallel Roads will find a clear summary by J. B. Sissons in a booklet published by the Nature Conservancy Council. A more detailed paper by the same author can be found in *Transactions of the Institute of British Geography, New Series* 4 (1) 1979.

Transport and Accommodation

The West Highland Railway between Glasgow and Fort William has stations at Tulloch and Roy Bridge and a post-bus operates between Roy Bridge and Moy. This latter service meets the north-bound morning train—telephone 039 781 235. Bunkhouse accommodation at Fersit and camp-sites at Roy Bridge are detailed in chapter 11 (see pp. 155–6). Those wishing to camp at Aberarder should seek permission at the farm of that name. Those wishing to use the bothy of Luib-chonnal in the stalking season should first contact Mr. R. J. Tapp at Braeroy Lodge— telephone 039 781 210.

References

Rock and Ice Climbs in Lochaber and Badenoch, A. C. Stead (SMC) 1981.

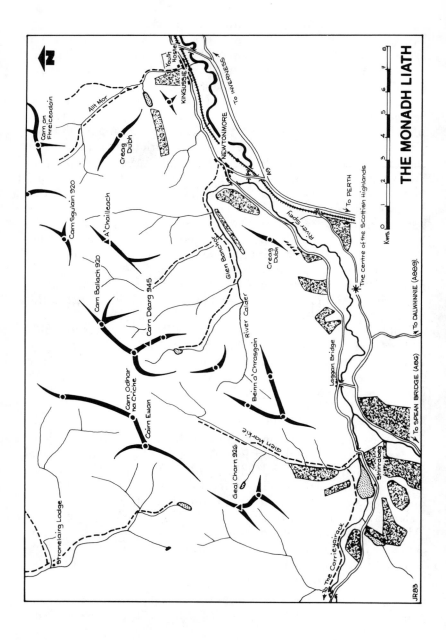

THE MONADH LIATH

The centre of the Scottish Highlands

JR83

184

15

Monadh Liath
and the Corrieyairack

*Geall Charn (926 m) 561988
*Carn Dearg (945 m) 635024
 Carn Macoul (800 m) 640005
 Carn Ban (942 m) 632031
 Carn Balloch (920 m) 643045
*Carn Sgulain (920 m) 684059
*A'Chailleach (930 m) 681041
 Corrieyairack Hill (896 m) 429998
 Cairn Chuilinn (816 m) 416034
 Meall an L'Aisre (862 m) 515000
 Carn na Saobhaidhe (811 m) 600145
 Carn an Fhreiceadain (878 m) 726071
 Geal-charn Mor (824 m) 837124

Sheets 34 and 35 Second Series O.S. 1:50,000

In any guide treating topography with anything wider than a
singular bias toward distinctive hill-form above 900 m, this
enormous tract of high land, making up perhaps a quarter of the
total area of the Central Highlands, would deserve several
chapters. However the fact is that relative to all other areas in
this guide, the Monadh Liath can best be described as featureless. Certainly there are few summits over 900 m and these are
clustered in the south-east corner, while to the north extensive
high moorland of blanket peat-bog between 700 and 800 m is
broken only by long, deeply-cut glens. Extensive carpets of grey
woolly hair moss cover the higher ground but the corries above
Glen Banchor are rich in the dwarf plants of alpine lady's
mantle, tormentil and alpine cinquefoil.

So featureless is the northern moorland and so many are the
Carn Deargs and the Carn Saobhaidhes that six-figure grid-
references are given in the chapter heading. The limits of the area

have been taken as the Corrieyairack Pass and Spey Valley in the south and the Great Glen and the A9 west and east respectively.

Wade's route across the Corrieyairack was no innovation—it had been in use much earlier by drovers and was shown on a map dated 1725 (in the British Museum)—and its hard surface was detested by former users whose cattle fared badly on the hard stones lacking gravel in-fill. (Later Thomas Telford, aware of just this problem, was to insist on a minimum of 14 inches depth of gravel on his own roads). It was completed in 1731 and so well were the twelve zig-zags beneath the summit surveyed that their course is still in existence today. Two of Wade's bridges have also withstood two and a half centuries with very little maintenance in the last 100 years: they are at Garva Bridge and at the crossing of the Allt Coire Uchdachan; though, a little beyond the latter bridge, the roaring flood coursing down the Allt Lagan a'Bhainne took away first the original bridge and then a replacement of 1932 installed with funds from the Scottish Rights of Way Society. The current Bailey bridge was constructed by the Royal Engineers in 1961. Countless feet have crossed the Corrieyairack but one user whose feat must vie with the devotion of Clement Wragge and his daily ascent of Ben Nevis, is the minister of Laggan whose courtship with the eventual Mrs. Grant toward the end of the 18th century involved a return journey of c. 90 km, as she lived in Fort Augustus.

From the Great Glen a track starts through indigenous woodland 200 m west of Ardachy Lodge and keeps close to the burn past the fine series of waterfalls on the Culachy Burn. In the east the Corrieyairack road has a tarmacadam surface from Laggan on the A86 to Melgarve and a car driven this far gives good access to some of the lesser hills. While it is feasible to walk over all the Monadh Liath Munros in one, long day such an outing should be reserved for the end of a drought, as there are great, intervening distances over peat-hag. This long round would also miss some of the best features to be found in the southern glens and corries.

A'Chailleach is easily reached from Newtonmore and a car can be driven for 2 km up the steep road leading north-west from the village to the mouth of Glen Banchor. This unexpectedly open strath steeply contained on one side by the northern wall of Creag Dubh and on the other by a series of spurs, is a sheltered and fertile sanctuary for both birdlife and for men's cattle. Mrs. Grant, when married to her Laggan minister, recorded in her collected letters (*Letters from the Mountains*, 1801) the 'nomadic flitting' each early summer to shielings above Glen Banchor. Then in early spring osyter-catchers, curlews, lap-wings and sand-pipers will be found in unusual quantity.

Beside a small plantation of conifers at the narrow entrance to the glen there is space to leave a car and beyond the track leads west across the Allt a'Choarainn to the Allt Fionndrigh where it turns north and runs up the glen for 3 km. Where the track dwindles to a path and crosses the burn, a steep nose drops from the north-east and ascent of 200 m leads to easier going across Geall Charn (891 m) and on to A'Chailleach. Views from this ridge across the Spey Valley to the Cairngorms are particularly fine. Return can be varied by descending the open slopes due south veering south-east lower down to follow a burn past a bothy (687023) to a ford (692014) across the Allt a'Choarainn and a track down to Glen Banchor.

Carn Sgulain makes an obvious continuation from A'Chailleach with descent between the two of only 100 m. However unless the former makes part of a circuit around the head of Glen Banchor's northern feeders, it has nothing to recommend it and is moated by a series of peat hags that contain in their trenches an especially glutinous mud. The westerly route from Carn Sgulain over Meall a'Bhothain (909 m) and Carn Ballach (920 m) is featureless and the remains of a fence marking the district boundary and reaching to Carn Ban (942 m), is a welcome aid to navigation in thick weather.

Carn Dearg is the culminating point on a h gh ridge carrying other tops, sharply defined to the south and ending at Carn Macoul (800 m) and merging with the high moorland to the north at Carn Ban. The track through Glen Ban hor follows the River Calder and has bridges across both the Allt Fionndrigh and the Allt Ballach, so leading to the flats beneath Carn Macoul's south-east nose—a steep ascent for 200 m but leading to a fine ridge, and a natural circuit of some variety hinging on the stony top of Carn Ban, continuing over the barely perceptible top of Snechdach Slinnean (919 m and one of the tops of most dubious value entered in Sir Hugh Munro's original list: its highest point was once claimed to be under water—there is a tiny lochan on the summit—and, appropriately, it is no longer noted by name on the O.S. 1:50,000 map) and turning south to finish over the shapely cone of Carn Leth-choin (843 m). An evening descent of the latter top's east ridge with bars of sunshine flooding through the gaps in Glen Banchor's southern wall is a memorable experience.

Directly beneath Carn Dearg's summit cairn a buttress drops steeply for 100 m and though the mica-schist itself is not continuous enough for worthwhile climbing, a steep, shallow gully splits the east-facing buttress. In good winter conditions this gully is a pleasant climb at about Grade II. Perhaps the best approach is by the track up Gleann Fionndrigh and over the bealach between Creag Liath (745 m) and Meall na Ceardaich (870 m). From 50 m north of this bealach a terrace runs past grouse butts and through a boulder field to the head of Gleann Ballach: this approach offers a good view of the buttress. If descending in winter to the head of Gleann Ballach a careful line should be picked from Carn Dearg, first north for 400 m then north-east, in order to avoid a scarped ramp.

Geal Charn is separated from the other Monadh Liath tops by the long trench of Glen Markie and by 12 km of moorland peat-hags for those intent on following the high ground north-east over Cairn Ewen (875 m) and Carn Odhar na Criche (897 m). From Laggan the motorable road to Crathie, and on to the Corrieyairack, is a picturesque approach winding through farmsteads and beside the infant Spey with heavily wooded tors hemming in the strath. One of these tors carries the prehistoric hill fort of Dun-da-Lamh which is in a truly commanding position: it can be approached by a Forestry track leading from the road bend 200 m south of the bridge over the Spey. Where the road crosses the Spey near Crathie a track continues on the north side of the river to the Spey Dam and from there turns north up Glen Markie. This track was once an alternative drove road to that of the Corrieyairack and crossed the plateau at 830 m by the course of the Allt nam Beith to descend then to Loch na Lairig and Sronlairig Lodge. Glen Markie is incised along a fault line, that continues north of the plateau along the course of the Abhainn Cno Clach and, in its higher reaches, becomes a splendid ravine that makes an entertaining summer scramble. The Glen Markie track runs almost to its head—for c. 10 km with the upper half a path—and crosses the burn east of Geal Charn. In winter this crossing is en route for the fine corrie above Lochan a'Choire, the headwall of which is a steep crag beneath Geal Charn. The gully near the centre of the crag makes a straightforward winter ascent amongst splendid scenery.

In summer the Glen Markie track makes a less convenient approach for, the Markie Burn must be forded just beyond the afforestation on the west bank in order to reach easy slopes on the satellite top of Beinn Sgiath (887 m). Not often can a crossing be made here dry-shod and a better approach is from Sherramore (4 km west of Crathie) onto the open slopes south of the satellite top. By either route it is worth diverting to look into the curious trench of An Dirc Mhor, and higher, the gap between the Beinn Sgiath and Geal Charn is an ice-carved window—Uinneag a'Choire Lochain.

Creag Dubh

Only a few minutes from the main road (A86) and equidistant from Laggan and Newtonmore, there is a major crag. Creag Dubh has over 100 routes of up to 140 m in length: most are at or above the Very Severe standard and the rock is schist, broken with bands of white quartzite. The crag has a pastoral setting above birch woods, lochans and the infant Spey. Facing south-east and with a relatively low altitude, climbing is often possible when the high crags are wet and cold. Two guide books cover the crag and are complementary to each other, the first by D. Cuthbertson being comprehensive, having seven photo-diagrams and other photographs of climbing action; while the second by A. C. Stead is selective, has five line-diagrams and a different set of climbing action photographs. *Creag Dubh and Craig-a-Barns*, Dave Cuthbertson, (SMC) 1983; *Rock and Ice Climbs in Lochaber and Badenoch*, A. C. Stead (SMC) 1981.

Scattered over the northern wastes are some tops that fall within the list of hills over 2500 ft originally devised by J. Rooke Corbett. None is completely in the hinterland but **Carn na Saobhaidhe** (811 m) will require a certain level of devotion to Mr. Rooke Corbett's list since by either northern or western routes there is a walking distance of some 28 km for the return trip. The hill could be reached from Strath Dearne to the north-east but even Mr. Rooke Corbett, who was a very powerful walker, might have considered such a length of approach as gilding a rather wan lily! Both western and northern routes start from the B862/B851 road between Fort Augustus and Strath Nairn and for those not travelling by car there is a bus service from Inverness through Strath Nairn to Whitebridge on the River Foyers. This service runs Monday to Saturday all year but for current bus times the Inverness office of Highland Omnibuses should be contacted—telephone 0463 31816/33371. Local services radiating for short distances about Errogie and Whiteridge and using 4-seater Land Rovers are operated by the Post Office—telephone 045-63 201 (Gorthleck P.O.).

The western route starts at Bunkegivie at the foot of Loch Mhor and follows the track on the north side of the River E for 9 km to a ruin under a false Carn na Saobhaidhe (602 m). A further 5 km on slopes at very low angle lead to the top, from where the prospect around the compass is of featureless moor. The northern route uses the track running south to Dunmaglass Lodge and then up the Allt Uisg an t'Sidhein and has the merit of a good track to within 2 km of the top.

Geal-charn Mor (824 m) is easily reached from Lynwilg on the A9 2 km south of Aviemore. A good track from the northern end of the hamlet runs west through fine indigenous woods and can be followed up to 700 m. There is an Ordnance Survey cairn on the summit which commands a good view down Glen Feshie and across to the Cairngorms.

Carn an Fhreichaidean (878 m) is also served by an excellent track that reaches to a point at 750 m on the south ridge. This ancient track, shown on Roy's Map of 1755 follows the course of the Allt Mor from the centre of Kingussie and continues across the moor to upper Strath Dearne; however once past Carn an Fhreichaidean the path fades and only traces remain across Bruach nan-Imirichean and down the Allt Glas a'Charbaid.

Three of these minor tops lie close together and north of the Corrieyairack road between Garva Bridge and the road summit. **Meall na h'Aisre**, the most easterly, is best reached from Garva Bridge, where the stands of Scots pine complement the solid grace of Wade's double-arched bridge. A good path starts from the west side of the bridge and crosses then recrosses the burn within the first kilometre. Above, open slopes lead north over a satellite at 844 m and then north-west to the Ordnance Survey cairn. A zig-zag course of c. 8 km could be taken west to **Gairbeinn** (896 m) but would involve rough going over wet ground, and this top is easily reached from the Corrieyairack road east of Melgarve. From Gairbeinn a traverse to **Corrie-yairack Hill** is an attractive proposition, for though the eastern slopes fall steeply and there is an intermediate top—yet another Geal Charn (876 m)—to be traversed, the ground is well drained and the bealachs notably lacking in the morass of peat-hags so common on the Monadh-Liaths. There is also a fine downward view onto Loch an Aonaich Odhair from Geall Charn's north-western shoulder. Descent south from Corrieyairack Hill leads past the site of an ancient well at 424985.

The last of these minor tops and decidedly the most interesting, **Cairn Chuilinn** (816 m), is best reached by way of a good track leaving the A862 a little over 3 km from Fort Augustus at 402091. After 3½ km the track turns through 180° to cross the Allt Doe and at this point a path cuts off to the south. When the path runs out under steeper slopes it is worthwhile bearing south-south-east to a subsidiary top at 781 m from where Cairn Chuilinn stands out as a bold, craggy mass immediately above a tangle of lochans to the south. From Cairn Chuilinn itself the view is very fine: to the west the eye can follow the length of Loch Garry out to Knoydart and to the north a desolation of knob and lochan territory now patched with acres of conifers runs above the great trench of Loch Ness. Even though it involves some very rough going, the circuit from Cairn Chuilinn to Coire Doe via the well-named Garbh Choire (rough corrie) at the head of Glen Tarff is strongly recommended to those with a taste for hidden corners and wild, craggy ravines.

Indeed it is the glens that provide the most memorable features in the northern area which is a classic example of the dissected plateau left by glaciation. The longest glen, Strath Dearn writhes into the heart of the high moor and, with a little licence, could be considered to breach the plateau spine up the course of the Abhainn Cno Clach. A well maintained road runs from Tomatin to Coignafearn, and a post bus—a 4-seater Land Rover—makes an all year service (telephone Tomatin 080 82 201). At Coignafearn, numerous spurs have been planed off leaving steep noses above the flat bed of the glen, where the River Findhorn has cut its way through thick glacial gravels. All about the road end are sheilings bearing the prefix to their names of 'Coig' which signifies a measure of land or a fifth, from the old Celtic custom of dividing land into five parts, and, higher in the glen the ruins of crofts show that cultivation must have been taken to unusual altitudes. On a very much lesser scale two glens to the west are worth a visit. At Whitebridge on the A862 the glen occupied by the River Fechlin twists south-east to Loch Killin. This stretch of water is hemmed in by steep slopes, those to the east dropping precipitously into the loch and those to the west just allowing room for the track that continues to Sronlairig Lodge and can be followed through to Laggan—though there are 6 km with little trace of the old drove route over the plateau spine before the southern Glen Markie is reached. There is a post-bus service between Whitebridge and Killin Lodge— telephone Gorthleck P.O. 045 63 201.

Then further north Conagleann lies 2 km east of Loch Mhor and this narrow cleft through the hills has a fine granite crag with good rock-climbing, on its western flank. The crag is most quickly reached by the track from the B862 to Wester Aberchalder. Conagleann is one of the many fine features on the shelf that runs along the east side of Loch Ness and those with the leisure to wander, preferably on a bicycle, through the numerous lanes will find a great variety of lochs and glacially scoured crags. Loch Ness itself occupies the site of a wrench-fault first formed some 300 million years ago that has been scoured out to a consistent depth of 160 m for much of its 37 km length. This wrench fault is still unstable, minor tremors being recorded in the area during this century and earlier, in 1775 a considerable disturbance to the waters of the Great Glen were caused by the same earth movement that devastated Lisbon. Robert Southey in his *Journal of a Tour in Scotland in 1819*, recounts how the waters were driven 200 yards up the River Oich and overflowed the banks by 30 ft. Great movements along the line of the fault in ancient times has been shown by demonstrating that granite, at Foyers on Loch Ness and at Strontian 105 km south were once part of the same geological unit. Loch Ness was also the subject of a prophecy by the Brahan Seer (Conneach Odhar) who about 1650 promised that 'full-rigged ships will be seen sailing eastwards and westwards by the back of Tomnahurich' (i.e. from Inverness into the Great Glen). In the 1820's, when the Caledonian Canal was completed, his prophecy came to pass.

Accommodation

For an area of this size, there is a narrow choice of centres from which to operate. In the east there are Youth Hostels at Kingussie and Aviemore and information as to other (and ample) accommodation and campsites is best obtained from the Spey Valley Tourist Office—telephone Aviemore 810363. In the west Fort Augustus is the only centre providing accommodation.

References

Letters from the Mountains, Mrs. Grant, 1801.
Creag Dubh and Craig-a-Barns, Dave Cuthbertson, (SMC) 1983.
Rock and Ice Climbing in Lochaber and Badenoch, A. C. Stead, (SMC) 1981.

APPENDIX I

Mountain Names and Meanings

The following list attempts to give the meanings of the mountain names mentioned in the Guide. Gaelic spellings, as in the Guide itself, are those of the Ordnance Survey.

A'Chailleach: old wife.
Allt a' Mhuilinn: burn of the mill.
A'Mharconaich: the horse rider.
Am Bodach: the old man.
An Garbhanach: the rough ridge.
An Gearanach: the short ridge.
An t-Sròn: the nose.
Aonach Beag: little ridge.
Aonach Dubh: black ridge.
Aonach Eagach: notched ridge.
Aonach Mòr: great ridge.

Beinn a' Bheithir: peak of the thunderbolt.
Beinn a' Bhùiridh: hill of roaring (stags).
Beinn a' Chaoruinn: mountain of the rowan tree.
Beinn a' Chlachair: mason's mountain.
Beinn a' Chochuill: mountain of the cowl.
Beinn a' Chuallaich: mountain of herding.
Beinn Bheòil: mountain in the mouth (of Ben Alder).
Beinn Ceitlein: concealment, hill of
Beinn Chumhainn: narrow mountain.
Beinn Eibhinn: mountain with a fair outlook.
Beinn Eunaich: fowling peak.
Beinn Fhada: long mountain.
Beinn Fhionnlaidh: Finlay's mountain.
Beinn Iaruinn: iron mountain.
Beinn Maol Chaluim: Calum's bare mountain.
Beinn Mhic-Mhonaidh: mountain of the son of the moor.
Beinn Mholach: shaggy mountain.
Beinn nan Aighean: mountain of the hinds.
Beinn Sgulaird: large, old hat, hill of the
Beinn Teallach: forge, hill of the
Beinn Trilleachan: mountain of sandpipers.
Beinn Udlamain: mountain of the unsteady place.

194

Ben Alder: mountain of rock and water.
Ben Cruachan: mountain of peaks or stacks.
Ben Starav: stout mountain with small head.
Bidean nam Bian: peak of the bens.
Binnein Beag: little hill.
Binnein Mòr: big hill.
Buachaille Etive Beag: the little herdsman of Etive.
Buachaille Etive Mòr: the great herdsman of Etive.

Caisteal: the castle.
Càrn a' Chuilinn: cairn of the holly.
Càrn an Fhreiceadain: cairn of the watcher.
Càrn B(e)allach: cairn of the pass.
Càrn Bàn: white cairn.
Càrn Beag Dearg: little red cairn.
Càrn Dearg: red cairn.
Càrn Dearg Meadhonach: middle red cairn.
Càrn Easgann Bana: cairn of the white eels.
Càrn Liath: grey cairn.
Càrn Mòr Dearg: big red cairn.
Càrn na Laraiche Maoile: cairn of the bare site or ruin.
Càrn na Saobhaidhe: cairn of the fox's den.
Càrn Sgùlain: cairn of the basket.
Chno Dearg: red nut.
Clach Leathad: stony slope.
Creach Bheinn: mountain of prey or spoil.
Creag Dubh: black rock.
Creag Mhòr: great crag.
Creag Pitridh: crag of the hollow places?
Cruach Innse: stack of the meadow.

Diollaid a' Chàirn: saddle of the cairn.
Drochaid Glas: grey bridge.

Fara, The (G. faradh): ladder.
Fraochaidh: place of heather.

Gairbeinn: rough mountain.
Garbh Bheinn: rough mountain.
Geal-Chàrn: white cairn.
Geal-Chàrn Mòr: big white cairn.
Geàrr Aonach: short ridge.
Glas Bheinn: grey mountain.
Glas Bheinn Mhòr: big grey mountain.

Leum Uilleim: William's leap.

Mam Coire Easain: moor or plateau of the corrie of the waterfalls.

195

Mam na Gualainn: plateau of the shoulder.
Meall a' Bhùiridh: hill of the roaring (stags).
Meall an t-Snaim: hill of the knot.
Meall Cruidh: hill of the hardness.
Meall Cunail: seaward-looking hill (*Cuan*—ocean).
Meall Dearg: red hill.
Meall Garbh: rough hill.
Meall na h-Aisre: hill of the defile.
Meall na Leitreach: hill of slopes.
Meall nan Eun: hill of the birds.
Meall an t'Suidhe: hill of the sitting.
Meal Corronaich: hill of the bracken corrie.
Mullach Coire an Iubhair: top of the corrie of the yew tree.
Mullach Coire Choille-rais: top of the corrie of the shrub wood.
Mullach Coire nan Nead: top of the corrie of the nests.
Mullach nan Coirean: top of the corries.

Na Gruagaichean: the maidens.

Poite (Poit) Coire Ardair: pot of the high corrie.
Puist Coire Ardair: post of the high corrie.

Sgairneach Mhòr: big rocky hillside.
Sgòr Chòinnich: Kenneth's peak.
Sgòr Gaibhre: peak of the goats.
Sgòr Iutharn: hell's peak.
Sgòr na h-Ulaidh: peak of the hidden treasure.
Sgòr nam Fiannaidh: peak of the Fianns.
Sgòr an Iubhair: peak of the yew tree.
Sgòrr Bhan: white peak.
Sgòrr Dhearg: red peak.
Sgòrr Dhonuill: Donald's peak.
Sgùrr a' Bhuic: peak of the buck.
Sgùrr a' Mhaim: peak of the pass.
Sgùrr Chòinnich Beag: little mossy peak.
Sgùrr Chòinnich Mòr: big mossy peak.
Sgùrr Eilde Beag: little crag of the hinds.
Sgùrr Eilde Mòr: big crag of the hinds.
Sgùrr Innse: peak of the meadow.
Sne(a)chdach Slinnean: snowy shoulder-blade.
Sròn a' Ghearrain: nose of the gelding.
Sròn an Isean: nose of the gosling.
Sròn Coire na h-Iolaire: nose of the eagles' corrie.
Sròn Garbh: rough nose.
Sròn Garbh Choire: nose of the rough corrie.
Sròn nan Giubhas: nose of the firs.
Stob a' Bhruaich Lèith: peak of the grey brae.
Stob a' Choire Lèith: peak of the grey corrie.

Stob a' Choire Mheadhoin: peak of the middle corrie.
Stob a' Choire Odhair: peak of the dun corrie.
Stob a' Ghlais Choire: peak of the grey corrie.
Stob an Aonaich Mhòir: peak of the big ridge.
Stob an Cul Choire: peak at the back of the corrie.
Stob an Fhuarain: peak of the well.
Stob Bàn: white peak.
Stob Choire Dhuibh: peak of the black corrie.
Stob Coir' an Albannaich: peak of the corrie of the Scotsman.
Stob Coire Altruim: peak of the nursing corrie (hinds with calves).
Stob Coire a' Chairn: peak of the stony corrie.
Stob Coire an Easain: peak of the corrie of the waterfalls.
Stob Coire an Fhir Dhuibh: peak of the corrie of the black man.
Stob Coire an Laoigh: peak of the corrie of the calf.
Stob Coire Bhealaich: peak of the corrie of the pass.
Stob Coire Cath na Sine: peak of the corrie of the battle of storm.
Stob Coire Dheirg: peak of the red corrie.
Stob Coire Gaibhre: peak of the corrie of the goats.
Stob Coire Lèith: peak of the grey corrie.
Stob Coire nam Beith: peak of the corrie of the birch trees.
Stob Coire na Ceannain: peak of the corrie of the headland.
Stob Coire nan Lochan: peak of the corrie of the lochans.
Stob Coire Raineach: peak of the corrie of the ferns.
Stob Coire Sgreamhach: peak of the scabby corrie.
Stob Coire Sgriodain: peak of the scree corrie.
Stob Dearg: red peak.
Stob Diamh (Daimh): peak of the stags.
Stob Dubh: black peak.
Stob Garbh: rough peak.
Stob Ghabhar: peak of the goats.
Stob na Bròige: peak of the shoe.
Stob na Doire: peak of the copse.

Tom na Sròine: hill of the nose.

Uinneag a' Ghlas Choire: window of the grey corrie.

APPENDIX II

Selected Bibliography

Mountaineering

Avalanche Enigma, Colin Fraser, Murray.
The ABC of Avalanche Safety, ed. La Chapelle, obtainable from Glenmore Lodge.
Mountain Leadership, Eric Langmuir, Scottish Sports Council.
Scottish Mountains on Ski, Malcolm Slesser, West Col.
Always a Little Further, Alastair Borthwick, John Smith, 1983.
A Progress in Mountaineering, J. H. B. Bell (O.P.).
Mountaineering in Scotland and Undiscovered Scotland, W. H. Murray, Diadem compendium, 1982.
A Climber's Guide to Ben Nevis, G. G. MacPhee, (SMC) (O.P.).
A Climber's Guide to Ben Nevis, J. R. Marshall, (SMC) 1979.
Rock and Ice Climbs: Glencoe and Glen Etive, Ken Crocket, (SMC) 1980.
Rock and Ice Climbs in Lochaber and Badenoch, A. C. Stead and J. R. Marshall, (SMC) 1981.
Creag Dubh and Craig-a-Barns, Dave Cuthbertson, (SMC) 1983.

Early Travellers

Recollections of a tour made in Scotland A.D. *1803*, Dorothy Wordsworth, (James Thin) 1974.
Letters from the Mountains; 1773–1807, Mrs. Anne Grant of Laggan (O.P.).
Journal of a Tour in Scotland in 1819, Robert Southey (O.P.).
Prospects and Observations on a Tour in England and Scotland in 1785, Thomas Newte (O.P.).
Journal (Rev. J. B. Craven's edition), Bishop Robert Forbes (O.P.).

198

Weather

Climate and the British Scene, Gordon Manley, (Collins Fontana) 1962.
Britain's Weather: Its Workings, Lore and Forecasting, David Bowen, (David and Charles) 1973.

Flora and Fauna

The Highlands and Islands, F. Fraser Darling and J. Morton Boyd, (Collins) 1964.
A Herd of Red Deer, F. Fraser Darling, (O.U.P.) 1969.

Land-form

The Scenery of Scotland, A. Geike (O.P.).
Geology and Scenery in Scotland, J. B. Whittow, (Penguin) 1979.
British Regional Geology—Scotland: The Grampian Highlands, G. Scott Johnstone, (HMSO) 1966.

History

Montrose, John Buchan, (Nelson) 1928.
The Drove Roads of Scotland, A. R. B. Haldane, (Edinburgh University Press) 1968.
New Ways through the Glens, A. R. B. Haldane, (Nelson) 1962.
The Prophecies of the Brahan Seer, A. Mackenzie, (Golspie) 1970.

Novels and General

Kidnapped, Robert Louis Stevenson.
The New Road, Neil Munro, (Blackwood).
Children of the Dead End, Pat MacGill, (Caliban) 1982.
Twenty Years on Ben Nevis, Wm. T. Kilgour, (O.P.).
The High Tops of Black Mount, Marchioness of Breadalbane, (Blackwood, O.P.) 1935.
The Path by the Water, A. R. B. Haldane, (Nelson, O.P.) 1944.

INDEX

DISTRICT GUIDE BOOKS
TO SCOTLAND

Since the new series SMC district guide books commenced publication in 1968 many requests have been received for an outline of the divisions in Scotland covered by the main series of eight volumes. *Munro's Tables* and the *Mountains of Scotland* are additional volumes in the series covering the whole of Scotland in their respective subjects. The map reproduced on the opposite page shows the eight divisions represented by the main series.

The Scottish Mountaineering Club Journal, published annually in July, is a useful source of additional information about mountaineering in the areas covered by these Tables. Every year it describes new routes and first ascents and reports significant changes in mountain shelters, bridges, paths and general access, as well as alterations to designated mountain heights and the status of Munros and Tops.

AREAS COVERED BY S.M.C.
DISTRICT GUIDE BOOKS.

ISLANDS OF SCOTLAND

WICK

NORTHERN
HIGHLANDS

ULLAPOOL

INVERNESS

ISLAND
OF SKYE

WESTERN
HIGHLANDS

AVIEMORE

ABERDEEN

CENTRAL
HIGHLANDS

CAIRNGORMS

FORT WILLIAM

ISLANDS OF SCOTLAND

SOUTHERN
HIGHLANDS

GLASGOW

EDINBURGH

SOUTHERN

UPLANDS

JR'74

CENTRAL HIGHLANDS – NORTH

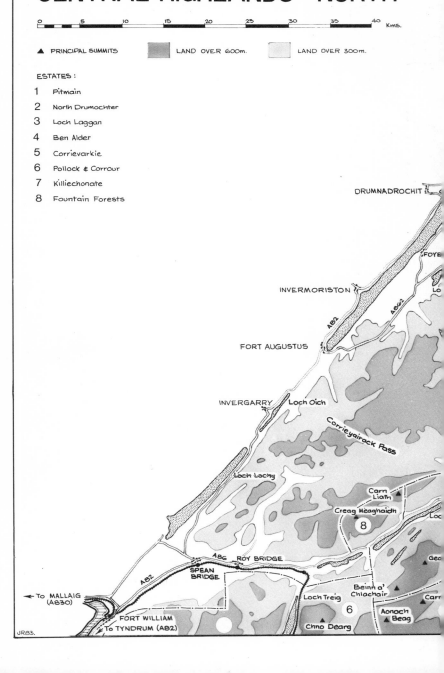

0 5 10 15 20 25 30 35 40 Kms.

▲ PRINCIPAL SUMMITS   LAND OVER 600m.   LAND OVER 300m.

ESTATES :

1 Pitmain
2 North Drumochter
3 Loch Laggan
4 Ben Alder
5 Corrievarkie
6 Pollock & Corrour
7 Killiechonate
8 Fountain Forests

DRUMNADROCHIT
FOYE
INVERMORISTON
FORT AUGUSTUS
A82
A862
Lo
INVERGARRY   Loch Oich
Corrieyairack Pass
Loch Lochy
Carn Liath ▲
Creag Meaghaidh ▲
(8)
Loc
A86 ROY BRIDGE
SPEAN BRIDGE
A82
Geo
←To MALLAIG (A830)
A82
Beinn a' Chlachair ▲
Carr
Loch Treig
(6)
Aonach Beag ▲
FORT WILLIAM
To TYNDRUM (A82)
Chno Dearg

JR83.